Microsoft
Pocket
Guide

Microsoft
Excel 2000

Microsoft Office Application

PUBLISHED BY
Microsoft Press
A Division of Microsoft Corporation
One Microsoft Way
Redmond, Washington 98052-6399

Library of Congress Cataloging-in-Publication Data
Nelson, Stephen L., 1959-
     Microsoft Pocket Guide to Microsoft Excel 2000 / Stephen L.
Nelson.
          p. cm.
     Includes index.
     ISBN 1-57231-971-2
     1. Microsoft Excel (Computer file)   2. Electronic spreadsheets.
I. Title
HF5548.4.M523N456   1999
005.369--dc21

                                        98-44769
                                        CIP

Printed and bound in the United States of America.

1 2 3 4 5 6 7 8 9   MLML   4 3 2 1 0 9

Distributed in Canada by ITP Nelson, a division of Thomson Canada Limited.

A CIP catalogue record for this book is available from the British Library.

Microsoft Press books are available through booksellers and distributors worldwide. For further information about international editions, contact your local Microsoft Corporation office or contact Microsoft Press International directly at fax (425) 936-7329. Visit our Web site at mspress.microsoft.com.

Acquisitions Editor: Susanne M. Forderer
Project Editor: Anne Taussig

Microsoft
Pocket
Guide

Microsoft
Excel 2000

Microsoft Office Application

Stephen L. Nelson　　　**Microsoft** Press

The Microsoft Pocket Guide to Microsoft Excel 2000 *is divided into five sections. These sections are designed to help you find the information you need quickly.*

1 Environment

Terms and ideas you'll want to know to get the most out of Microsoft Excel 2000. All the basic parts of Excel are shown and explained. The emphasis here is on quick answers, but many topics are cross-referenced so that you can find out more if you want to.

Diagrams of key components, with quick definitions, cross-referenced to more complete information.

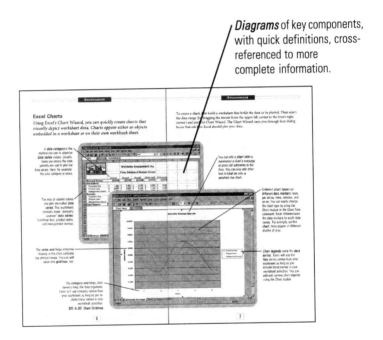

Tips

Watch for these as you use this Pocket Guide. They'll point out helpful hints and let you know what to watch for.

13 Excel A to Z

An alphabetic list of commands, tasks, terms, and procedures.

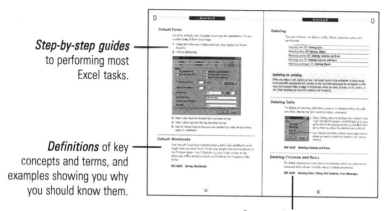

Step-by-step guides to performing most Excel tasks.

Definitions of key concepts and terms, and examples showing you why you should know them.

Cross-references to related topics.

151 Troubleshooting

A guide to common problems—how to avoid them, and what to do when they occur.

165 Quick Reference

Useful indexes, including a full list of menu commands, toolbar buttons, and more.

181 Index

A complete reference to all elements of the Pocket Guide.

Introduction

This Pocket Guide provides quick, practical answers to just about any question you have about Microsoft Excel 2000. To acquaint yourself with this convenient and easy-to-use book, take two minutes now and read the Introduction. It explains how this unusual little book works.

What Is a Pocket Guide?

One of the problems with the larger books about computers is, quite frankly, their size. With a large book, you must typically sift through pages of information to find that one piece of information you need. Not only that, you have to contend with their physical size. It's rarely enjoyable and often not practical to lug around a thousand-page book if you're working both at home and at the office, or if you're on the road with your laptop.

The *Microsoft Pocket Guide to Microsoft Excel 2000* addresses both "size" problems of the larger computer books. Most obvious, of course, is the fact that this book is smaller. So it's easier to carry the book around wherever you go.

But this Pocket Guide also addresses the problem of wading through a large book to find the piece of information you need. And it does so in a variety of ways. For starters, this Pocket Guide organizes its information using an A to Z scheme—just like a dictionary or an encyclopedia does. This Pocket Guide supplies visual indexes in its Environment section, so you can find help even if you don't know how to describe what it is you're looking for. Finally, this Pocket Guide also uses a rich cross-referencing scheme that points you to related topics.

For new users, the Pocket Guide provides the essential information necessary to start using Excel. And for experienced users, the Pocket Guide provides concise, easy-to-find descriptions of Excel tasks, terms, and techniques.

When You Have a Question

Let me explain how to find the information you need. If Excel is new to you, flip first to the Environment section, which is a visual index. Find the picture that shows what you want to do or the task you have a question about. If you want to build a worksheet, for example, flip to pages 4 and 5, which show a worksheet.

Next read the captions that describe the parts of the picture. Say, for example, that you want to build a sales budget. The worksheet on pages 4 and 5 includes captions that describe how to enter textual descriptions and budgeted values. You'll notice that some captions use **boldface** terms or are followed by boldface terms. These refer to entries in the second section, Excel A to Z, which provide more information related to the caption's contents.

Excel A to Z is a dictionary of more than 200 entries that define terms and describe tasks. (After you've worked with Excel a little or if you're already an experienced user, you'll often be able to turn directly to that section.) So if you have just read the caption that says you can enter **formulas** into a worksheet, you can flip to the Formulas entry in Excel A to Z.

When an entry in Excel A to Z appears as a term within another entry, I'll often **boldface** it the first time it appears in that entry. For example, as part of describing how formulas work, I might tell you that formulas can use a **cell address**. In this case, the words "cell address" appear in bold letters—alerting you to the presence of a Cell Address entry in the second section. If you don't understand the term or want to do some brushing up, you can flip to the entry for more information.

When You Have a Problem

The third section, Troubleshooting, describes problems that new or casual users of Excel often encounter. Following each problem description, I list one or more solutions that you can employ to fix the problem.

When You Wonder About a Command

The Quick Reference at the end of the Pocket Guide describes Excel's menu commands and the **toolbar** buttons. If you want to know what a specific command or toolbar button does, turn to the Quick Reference. Don't forget about the index either. You can look there to find all references to any single topic in this book.

Conventions Used Here

I have developed a few conventions to make using this book easier for you. Rather than use wordy phrases such as "Activate the File menu and then choose the Print command" to describe how you choose a menu command, I'm just going to say, "Choose the File menu's Print command."

Here's another convention: To make dialog box button and box labels stand out, I've capitalized the initial letter of each word in the label. I think this makes it easier to understand an instruction such as "Select the Print To File check box." With this scheme, it's easier to see, for example, that "Print To File" is a label.

One final point: In general, I try to tell you the easiest, most direct way to get things done. For example, I'll often suggest you use **shortcut menu** commands or toolbar buttons instead of conventional menu commands. I also assume you know how to select menu commands, windows, and dialog box elements by using either the mouse or the keyboard.

Environment

Need to get oriented
quickly? Then the
Environment is the place
to start. It defines the key
terms you'll need to know
and the core ideas you
should understand as
you begin exploring
Microsoft Excel 2000.

Excel's Program Window

When you start Microsoft Excel 2000, Windows displays the Excel program window, which contains an empty, ready-to-use workbook.

The *menu bar* lists the Excel menus, which include the commands you use to build, **print**, and save your workbooks. Excel customizes the menus as you work, removing and adding commands based on the work you do.
SEE ALSO **Saving Workbooks**

The *program window* provides a menu bar and displays Excel **workbooks.**

Toolbars contain buttons that you use in place of often-needed menu commands.
SEE ALSO **Formatting; Personal Menus and Toolbars**

A *cell* is created by the intersection of a column and a row. You identify a cell by its column letter and row number. Cell A1, for example, appears at the intersection of column A and row 1.
SEE ALSO **Cell Address**

Click *page tabs* to display a particular page. Use the Page buttons to flip through the sheets in a workbook or to jump to the first or last sheet in a workbook.
SEE ALSO **Sheets**

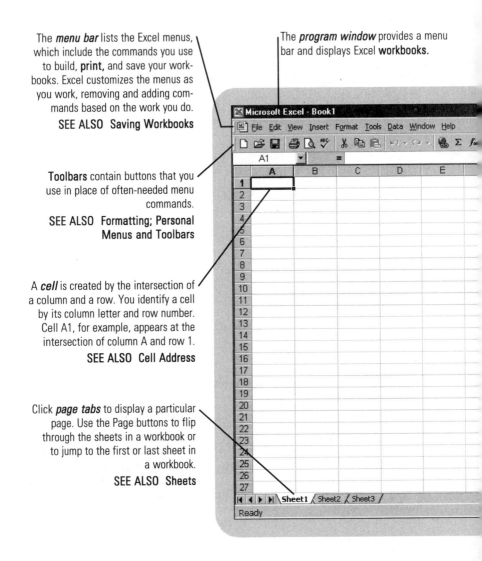

Workbooks are stacks of **worksheets** and **chart sheets**. A workbook is analogous to a pad of spreadsheet paper. On the pages, or sheets, of the workbook, you enter data, and then you can use that data to plot charts. Only a portion of a single worksheet is visible at one time.

Worksheets are organized into lettered **columns** and numbered **rows**. A worksheet has 256 columns and 16,384 rows—plenty of room for even very large and very complex financial reports.

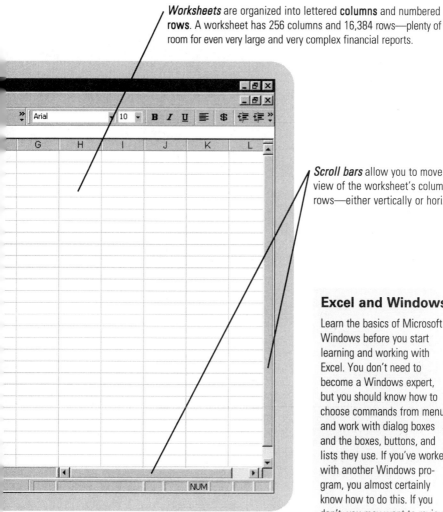

Scroll bars allow you to move your view of the worksheet's columns and rows—either vertically or horizontally.

Excel and Windows

Learn the basics of Microsoft Windows before you start learning and working with Excel. You don't need to become a Windows expert, but you should know how to choose commands from menus and work with dialog boxes and the boxes, buttons, and lists they use. If you've worked with another Windows program, you almost certainly know how to do this. If you don't, you may want to review the Windows tutorial or your Windows documentation.

Excel Worksheets

Worksheets are the basic building blocks of workbooks. By entering information for labels, values, and formulas into worksheet cells, you create tables, or spreadsheets, useful for summarizing, tabulating, and analyzing.

Formulas can add, subtract, multiply, and divide values. Usually, these values are stored in another cell. To get a value stored in a cell, the formula uses the **cell's address**. This formula adds the values in cells B9, B10, B11, B13, B14, and B15.

Labels are pieces of text. Often, you use labels to describe values stored in other cells.

Numeric punctuation—dollar signs, commas, and decimal places—makes worksheet values easier to read.

SEE ALSO Formatting

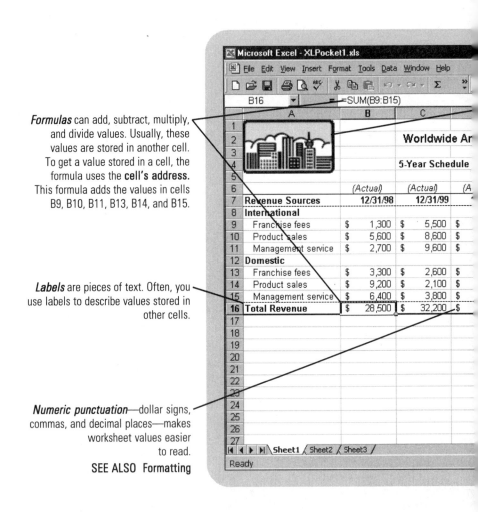

To build a **worksheet,** simply enter **labels, values,** and **formulas** in the cells. To do this, click the cell, type what you want, and then press Enter. The unique feature of a spreadsheet program such as Excel is its ability to calculate formulas. When you enter a formula in a worksheet cell, Excel calculates the formula's result. If the formula uses values from other cells—the usual case—Excel recalculates the formula's result any time one of these values changes.

SEE ALSO Calculating Formulas

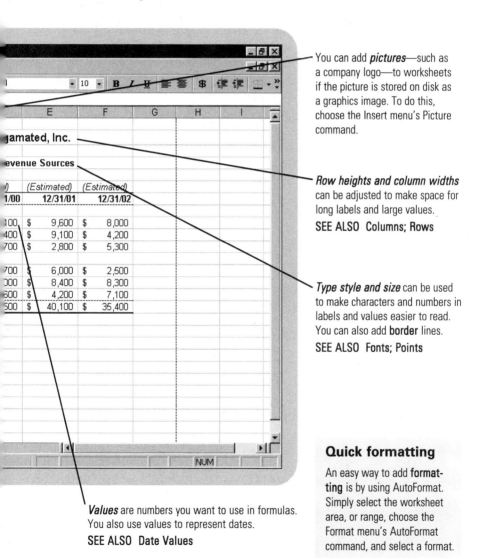

You can add *pictures*—such as a company logo—to worksheets if the picture is stored on disk as a graphics image. To do this, choose the Insert menu's Picture command.

Row heights and column widths can be adjusted to make space for long labels and large values.
SEE ALSO Columns; Rows

Type style and size can be used to make characters and numbers in labels and values easier to read. You can also add **border** lines.
SEE ALSO Fonts; Points

Quick formatting

An easy way to add **formatting** is by using AutoFormat. Simply select the worksheet area, or range, choose the Format menu's AutoFormat command, and select a format.

Values are numbers you want to use in formulas. You also use values to represent dates.
SEE ALSO Date Values

5

Excel Charts

Using Excel's Chart Wizard, you can quickly create charts that visually depict worksheet data. Charts appear either as objects embedded in a worksheet or on their own workbook sheet.

A *data category* is the method you use to organize **data series** values. Usually, these are simply the time periods you use to plot the data series. Here, for example, the data category is years.

The sets of related values you plot are called *data series*. This worksheet provides three "domestic revenue" **data series:** franchise fees, product sales, and management service.

The *value axis* helps someone looking at the chart calibrate the plotted values. You can add value axis **gridlines,** too.

The *category axis* helps chart viewers keep the data organized. Excel will use category names from your worksheet as long as you include these names in your worksheet selection.

SEE ALSO Chart Gridlines

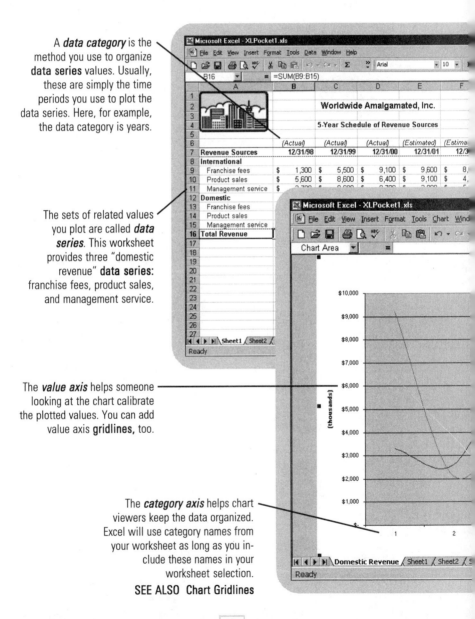

To create a **chart**, first build a **worksheet** that holds the data to be plotted. Then select the data range (by dragging the mouse from the upper left corner to the lower right corner) and start the Chart Wizard. The Chart Wizard steps you through four dialog boxes that ask how Excel should plot your data.

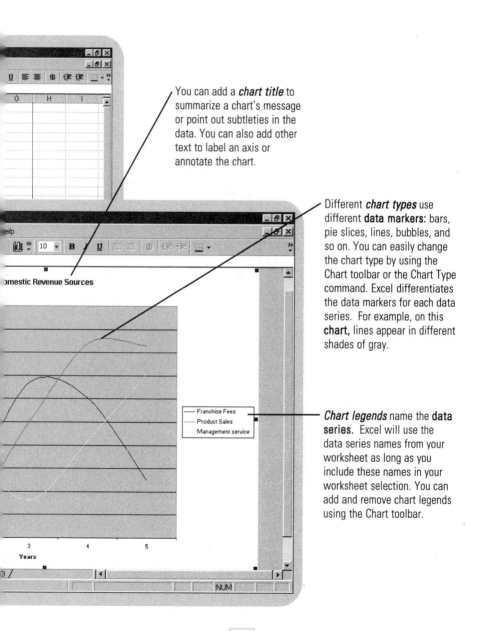

You can add a *chart title* to summarize a chart's message or point out subtleties in the data. You can also add other text to label an axis or annotate the chart.

Different *chart types* use different **data markers**: bars, pie slices, lines, bubbles, and so on. You can easily change the chart type by using the Chart toolbar or the Chart Type command. Excel differentiates the data markers for each data series. For example, on this **chart**, lines appear in different shades of gray.

Chart legends name the **data series**. Excel will use the data series names from your worksheet as long as you include these names in your worksheet selection. You can add and remove chart legends using the Chart toolbar.

List Management

List Management is a simple yet handy database feature.
A list is an organized set of similar blocks of information.

The first row names the **fields** of the list. Each column stores the same information: names in column A, departments in column B, and so on.

To **create a list,** you use the rows and columns of a worksheet. In this example, each employee goes into a separate row: Fùmio on the first row, Geoffrey on the second row, and so on.

This list shows only 14 entries, or **records,** and uses only 3 columns, even though an Excel worksheet provides 16,384 rows and 256 columns. So you can store very large lists in a worksheet if your computer has enough memory and disk space.

You can arrange, or **sort,** list entries. For example, you can alphabetize a list by employee names (as shown here). You can also organize a list in order of ascending or descending value fields (such as by salary).
SEE ALSO Sorting Lists

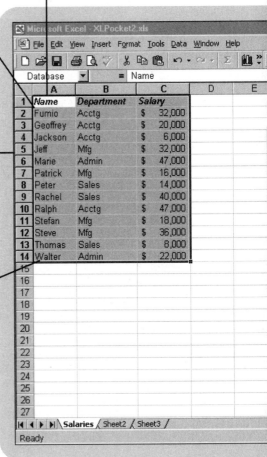

	A	B	C
1	**Name**	**Department**	**Salary**
2	Fumio	Acctg	$ 32,000
3	Geoffrey	Acctg	$ 20,000
4	Jackson	Acctg	$ 6,000
5	Jeff	Mfg	$ 32,000
6	Marie	Admin	$ 47,000
7	Patrick	Mfg	$ 16,000
8	Peter	Sales	$ 14,000
9	Rachel	Sales	$ 40,000
10	Ralph	Acctg	$ 47,000
11	Stefan	Mfg	$ 18,000
12	Steve	Mfg	$ 36,000
13	Thomas	Sales	$ 8,000
14	Walter	Admin	$ 22,000

To build a list, use a **worksheet.** Typically, you use a row for each list entry. Information stored in a list can be textual (for example, employee names) or numeric (for example, salary amounts). You can also include **formulas.**

You can enter data directly into the worksheet by clicking a **cell,** typing, and then pressing Enter or choosing the Data menu's Form command.

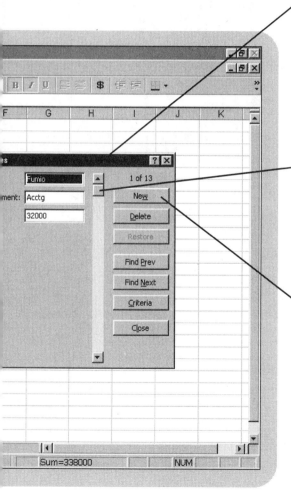

In the *Data Form dialog box,* you can enter and edit records in a list. To use it, select a list's headers and its entries and then choose the Data menu's Form command. Excel uses the worksheet name to name the dialog box, and it uses the column headings to label the text boxes in the dialog box.

To *edit the list entry* displayed, edit the text box contents and move to the next record. You can page through the list using the Up and Down arrow keys, the Find Next or Find Prev buttons, and the scroll bar.

Click New to *start a new list entry* with the Data Form dialog box, and then fill in the blank text boxes and move to the next record.

Publishing Excel Workbooks

You can publish Excel workbooks electronically on a web or simply by printing on paper.

Use a **web browser** to view work-books you publish as a web page. Some web browsers may even be able to edit the workbook.
SEE ALSO Office Server Extensions; Web Components

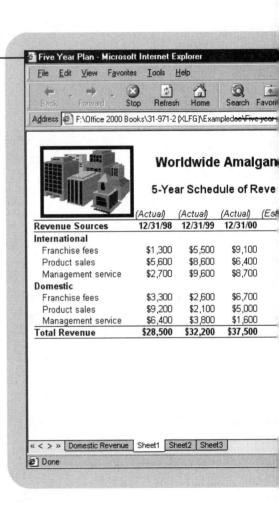

Previewing web pages

You can see what your workbook's web pages will look like without actually publishing them to a web server. To do so, choose the File menu's Web Page Preview command. Excel displays a web browser window that shows how the workbook will look as a web page.

To **print** a worksheet or a chart, choose the File menu's Print command. To publish a workbook on a web server, choose the File menu's Save As Web Page command. When you choose either command, Excel displays a dialog box that asks what and how you want to print or publish, but you can accept the default, or suggested, settings by pressing Enter or clicking OK.

SEE ALSO Saving Web Pages

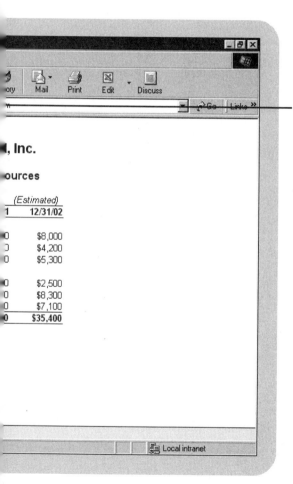

ory	Mail	Print	Edit	Discuss	

, Inc.

ources

	(Estimated)
1	12/31/02
0	$8,000
]	$4,200
0	$5,300
0	$2,500
0	$8,300
0	$7,100
0	$35,400

Local intranet

HTML is available as an Excel file format. This means you can store Excel documents as HTML files on a web server, making workbook sharing and collaboration easy.
SEE ALSO Saving Workbooks; Web Folders

Previewing printed pages

You can see what your printed pages will look like without actually printing them. To do so, choose the File menu's Print Preview command. Excel displays a window that shows a printed page and provides buttons you can use to page through the document, adjust page settings (such as margins and footers), and initiate printing once your pages look right.

Excel

A to Z

When you have a question,
you want a quick, easy
answer. Excel A to Z,
which starts on the next
page, should provide just
these sorts of answers. It
lists in alphabetic order
the tools, terms, and
techniques you'll need
to know.

Absolute Cell Address

An absolute cell address is simply a **cell address** you use in a formula but don't want adjusted when the formula is copied.

Creating Absolute Cell Addresses

Make the column and row components of a cell address absolute by preceding them with a dollar sign. For example, to make the cell address A1 absolute, insert dollar signs—A1.

Creating Mixed Cell Addresses

In a mixed cell address, only some components are absolute. To create a mixed cell address, simply precede those address components you want absolute with a dollar sign. For example, the cell address $A1 has only its column fixed, and the cell address A$1 has only its row fixed.

The absolute key

When editing or entering a cell address, you can select the address in the formula bar and then press F4 to change a cell address from relative to absolute, from absolute to mixed, and from mixed back to relative.

SEE ALSO Copying Formulas; Relative Cell Address

Active Cell

The active cell is the cell with the **cell selector,** or pointer (the dark-bordered box that jumps from cell to cell as you press direction keys). If you type something and press Enter, Excel puts what you type into the active cell. And the address of the active cell—the **cell reference**—shows in the Name box.

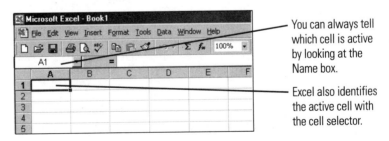

You can always tell which cell is active by looking at the Name box.

Excel also identifies the active cell with the cell selector.

Active Sheet

The active sheet is the one you can see in the workbook window. It's the sheet that selected commands act on. The active sheet also determines which menu bar Excel provides. For example, if a worksheet is active, Excel displays the worksheet menu bar; if a chart sheet is active, Excel displays the chart menu bar.

Adaptability

Excel customizes its menus and toolbars so they provide only the commands and tools you regularly use. This adaptability makes it easier for you to find the menu commands and toolbar buttons you use most.

You still have access to all of Excel's features even with Excel's adaptability, however. If you point to the double arrow at the bottom of a menu, or linger on a menu, Excel displays its long menus, which supply all the commands. And if you click the double arrow toolbar button, Excel displays an extended set of toolbar buttons.

SEE ALSO   Personal Menus and Toolbars

Adding Styles

A style is a combination of formatting choices. To add a style to an open workbook, format a cell so that it uses the style and then choose the Format menu's Style command.

1 Name the style in the Style Name drop-down list box.

2 The Style Includes section shows the formatting choices that make up the style. To remove formatting choices, click check boxes to clear them.

3 After you finish selecting all your formatting choices, click Add.

4 If you want to change a style, select it from the Style Name box, click Modify, and use the Format Cells dialog box that Excel displays.

continues

Adding Styles *(continued)*

Deleting styles

If you inadvertently add a style you don't want or if you no longer need a style, select it from the Style Name drop-down list box and then click Delete.

SEE ALSO Formatting

Aligning Labels and Values

Alignment refers to how Excel positions **labels** and **values** in cells. Unless you tell it otherwise, Excel applies two simple alignment rules: left-align labels, and right-align values. You can override these rules with the Format menu's Cells command. To do this, follow these steps:

1 Select the cell or cells.

2 Choose the Format menu's Cells command. Excel displays the Format Cells dialog box.

3 Click the Alignment tab.

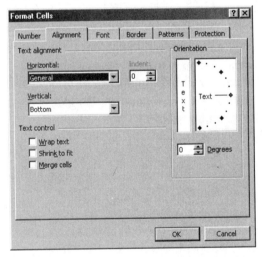

4 Select an option from the Horizontal drop-down list box and set an amount in the Indent box to indicate how labels and values should align with the left and right edges of cells:

Choice	Result
General	The usual two rules are applied.
Left (Indent)	Labels and values are left-aligned.
Center	Labels and values are centered between the left and right edges of cells.
Right	Labels and values are right-aligned.
Fill	Labels are repeated in a cell as many times as they will fit.
Justify	Row height is adjusted and labels are broken into multiple lines of text.
Center Across Selection	Labels and values are centered across the selected cells.

5 Select the Wrap Text check box if you want row heights adjusted and labels broken into lines of text. (This is sometimes called wordwrapping.)

6 Select the Shrink To Fit check box if you want to make a label fit in a cell without increasing the cell size.

7 Select the Merge Cells check box if you want to combine the selected cells into one, new cell.

8 Select an option from the Vertical drop-down list box to indicate how labels and values should be aligned with the top and bottom edges of cells:

Choice	Result
Top	Labels and values are aligned flush to top edge.
Center	Labels and values are centered between top and bottom edges.
Bottom	Labels and values are aligned flush to bottom edge.
Justify	Row height is adjusted so that labels can be broken into vertical lines of text.

9 Make adjustments in the Orientation boxes and set an amount in the Degrees box to indicate how labels and values should appear in cells.

10 Click OK.

Apple Macintosh

This book isn't about Excel for the Macintosh; it's about Excel for Microsoft Windows. But you may be interested to know that you can easily move spreadsheets from Excel for Windows to Excel for the Macintosh. The reason for this is that an Apple Macintosh converts IBM PC files, such as an Excel workbook, to equivalent Macintosh files, such as an Excel for the Macintosh workbook.

SEE ALSO Date Values

Applying Styles

To apply, or use, a style, follow these steps:

1 Select the cells you want to format.

2 Choose the Format menu's Style command. Excel displays the Style dialog box.

3 Select the style from the Style Name box.

4 If you don't want to use one of the formatting choices—Number, Alignment, Font, Border, Patterns, or Protection—clear its check box..

5 Click OK.

Painting styles

You can copy a style from one cell to another by using the Format Painter toolbar button. Select the cell with the style you want to copy. Click the Format Painter toolbar button. Then select the cell or range to which you want to copy the style.

SEE ALSO Formatting

Argument

An argument is a unit of information, or an input, used in a **function**. Arguments can be **labels**, **values**, **cell addresses**, cell names, **formulas**, and even other functions. Arguments are enclosed in parentheses and separated by commas. For example, the function that calculates a monthly loan payment uses a minimum of three inputs—the interest rate, the number of monthly payments, and the loan amount. If the annual interest rate is 8 percent, the number of years of monthly payments is 3, and the loan is $5000, you could enter the following function:

```
=PMT(.08/12,3*12,5000)
```

The annual interest rate is 8 percent, or .08; so the monthly interest rate argument is .08/12—the annual interest rate divided by 12. The loan requires monthly payments over 3 years; so the payments argument is 3*12, which returns the number of monthly payments made over 3 years. The last argument, 5000, is the loan amount.

A handful of functions don't use arguments, for example, the function for calculating the mathematical constant pi. When a function doesn't use arguments, follow the function name with empty parentheses, as shown below with the pi function:

```
=PI ()
```

Array

An array is a set of numbers—such as those stored in a row or a column. You can use arrays in **array formulas** to return other arrays. For example, you can add the array 1, 2, 3 to the array 4, 5, 6, and you get a new array—5, 7, 9.

Array 1:	1	2	3
+ Array 2:	4	5	6
= Array 3:	5	7	9

This makes sense, right? The first number in Array 3, 5, is calculated by adding the first numbers in the two input arrays, 1 and 4. The second number, 7, is calculated by adding the second numbers in the two input arrays, 2 and 5.

Array Formulas

With handy and powerful array formulas you can write a single formula that makes several calculations. Sure, this sounds complicated, but a quick example will show you the basics of **arrays** and array formulas. Take a peek at the following portion of a worksheet. Suppose, for the sake of illustration, that you want to multiply the values in each row of column A by the values in each row of column B. Multiplying the account balance in column A by the interest rate in column B, for example, would calculate the interest.

continues

Array Formulas *(continued)*

Writing an Array Formula

To create an array formula that makes this calculation, follow these steps:

	A	B	C
1	Balance	Rate	Interest
2	$ 10,000.00	2%	200
3	$100,000.00	3%	3000
4	$ 10,000.00	4%	400
5	$100,000.00	5%	5000
6			

1 Select C2:C5.

2 Type the equals sign, =.

3 Select A2:A5.

4 Type the multiplication sign, *.

5 Select B2:B5.

6 Press Shift+Ctrl+Enter.

Excel enters the formula {=A2:A5*B2:B5} into each of the cells in C2:C5. This array formula tells Excel, "Calculate C2 by multiplying A2 by B2, calculate C3 by multiplying A3 by B3, calculate C4 by multiplying A4 by B4, and calculate C5 by multiplying A5 by B5." Note that the arrays in an array formula must have the same number of values.

Editing an Array Formula

You edit an array formula in the same way you edit other formulas. For example, double-click one of the cells with the array formula; then make your changes. If you edit an array formula, Excel removes the braces as you edit; so press Shift+Ctrl+Enter when you're finished to tell Excel the formula is an array. When you edit one of the array formulas, Excel updates each of the formulas in the array.

About those braces

Note that you don't type the braces yourself to create an array formula; press Shift+Ctrl+Enter, and Excel adds the braces for you.

ASCII Characters

The ASCII character set consists of the characters you see on your keyboard plus a couple dozen other characters that you don't see, are unprintable, and you don't need to worry about anyway.

Excel provides text functions that manipulate ASCII characters, show which characters various ASCII codes represent, and show which ASCII codes return which characters.

As a general rule, you shouldn't have to worry all that much about ASCII characters if you're working with Excel. Why? Because you can type all the ASCII characters that you'll need with the keyboard.

SEE ALSO   Unicode

ASCII Text Files

An ASCII text file is a text file that uses only **ASCII characters.** You can import ASCII text files using the File menu's Open command. And this is relevant because many accounting programs create ASCII text files as a way to share information.

SEE ALSO   Delimited Text Files; Importing Text Files

Auditing Worksheets

In a worksheet, which values get used where can be perplexing. To ease the burden, Excel provides a set of error-checking tools, which you make available by choosing the Tools menu's Auditing command and then choosing one of the submenu's commands: Trace Precedents, Trace Dependents, and Trace Error. These commands let you visually inspect relationships between **formulas** and the **values** used in formulas.

Tracing Precedents

The Trace Precedents command draws a blue arrow from the cells addressed by the active cell's formula to the active cell.

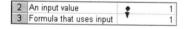

Tracing Dependents

You can see which cells depend on the active cell by using the Trace Dependents command. It draws a blue arrow from the active cell to cells addressing the active cell.

Tracing Errors

The Trace Error command draws arrows from cells addressed by an active cell's erroneous formula to the active cell. Excel draws red arrows from dependent cells holding error values; it draws blue arrows from all the other dependent cells.

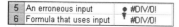

continues

Auditing Worksheets (continued)

Two More Tools

The Auditing submenu also provides two additional tools: Remove All Arrows, which erases the arrows you've added using the Trace commands; and Show Auditing Toolbar, which adds a toolbar for choosing auditing commands more quickly.

SEE ALSO Dependents; Error Messages; Precedents; Validation

AutoCalculate

AutoCalculate allows you to instantly calculate the values in the selected range. To use AutoCalculate, simply select a cell range. Six **functions** are available: AVERAGE, COUNT, COUNT NUMS, MAX, MIN, and SUM, with SUM as the default. Right-click in the AutoCalculate area to select the function you want to use.

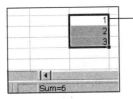 AutoCalculate shows the calculation result using the AutoCalculate area on the right side of the formula bar.

AutoComplete

When you type text in a cell, AutoComplete scans all entries in the same column and determines whether a possible match is in the column. If so, AutoComplete fills in the rest of the entry for you. For example, if a cell contains the text entry "Nails," and you begin typing "N" in the cell below, AutoComplete fills in the rest of the entry, "ails." If more than one entry in the column begins with "N," AutoComplete fills in the entry as soon as the nearest match is found.

AutoComplete matches only complete cell entries, not individual words in a cell. As soon as a unique match is found, AutoComplete suggests an entry. AutoComplete does not work when editing formulas. AutoComplete works only in contiguous ranges of cells.

Getting picky about AutoComplete

If AutoComplete is enabled—and by default it is—you'll see a Pick From List command on the **shortcut menu.** (The shortcut menu appears when you right-click a cell.) Choosing the Pick From List command displays a list of all the unique entries in adjacent cells in the same column. Selecting one of the entries in the list inserts it in the selected cell. You can disable AutoComplete by clicking the Tools menu's Options command, clicking the Edit tab, and then clearing the Enable AutoComplete For Cell Values check box.

AutoCorrect

AutoCorrect looks at the words you type and tries to fix all spelling and capitalization errors. For example, if you always misspell the word *the* as *teh*—perhaps your fingers fly just a bit too fast over the keys—AutoCorrect fixes your mistake. Automatically.

AutoFill SEE Fill Series

AutoFormatting Tables

You can format a worksheet selection, or range, to follow a conventional set of formatting rules. To do so, follow these steps:

1 Build the table, and then select it.

2 Choose the Format menu's AutoFormat command. Excel displays the AutoFormat dialog box.

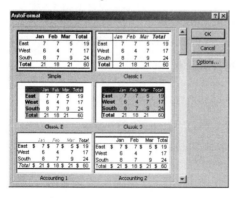

3 Click the table format that shows the formatting you want.

4 Click OK.

AutoSum

An autosum is simply a SUM() **function** you insert with the AutoSum tool.

Using the AutoSum Toolbar Button

Select the row, column, or range you want to sum, and then click the AutoSum toolbar button.

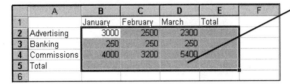

	A	B	C	D	E	F
1		January	February	March	Total	
2	Advertising	3000	2500	2300		
3	Banking	250	250	250		
4	Commissions	4000	3200	5400		
5	Total					
6						

Include an empty cell below each column you want to sum and to the right of each row you want to sum. Excel uses these empty cells for the new SUM() functions.

	A	B	C	D	E	F
1		January	February	March	Total	
2	Advertising	3000	2500	2300	7800	
3	Banking	250	250	250	750	
4	Commissions	4000	3200	5400	12600	
5	Total	7250	5950	7950	21150	
6						

Excel adds the SUM() functions to tally selected rows and columns. For example, in this cell, AutoSum adds the function **=SUM(B2:D2)**

Editing AutoSum Functions

You edit AutoSum functions in the same way you edit other formulas.

SEE ALSO   Math Functions

Bold Characters

You can make characters in the current worksheet selection **bold** by selecting the characters and then pressing Ctrl+B or clicking the Bold toolbar button. You can also choose the Format menu's Cells command and use its Font tab options.

SEE ALSO   Changing Fonts

Boolean Algebra

Boolean algebra, which you use in **conditional functions** and **filtering lists,** compares two values in a test question. If the test question answer is yes, the Boolean expression returns TRUE. If the test question answer is no, the expression returns FALSE. The following table shows some typical Boolean expressions:

Test	Question it asks
A1=B1	Is value in A1 equal to value in B1?
A1>B1	Is value in A1 greater than value in B1?
A1>=B1	Is value in A1 greater than or equal to value in B1?
A1<B1	Is value in A1 less than value in B1?
A1<=B1	Is value in A1 less than or equal to value in B1?
A1<>B1	Is value in A1 not equal to the value in B1?

The problem of precedence

The comparison operators used in a Boolean expression have lower precedence than the other arithmetic operations—such as exponentiation, multiplication and division, and addition and subtraction. In other words, the comparison calculation is the last calculation made in a formula that uses a Boolean expression.

SEE ALSO Formulas

Borders

You can add border lines to cells. To do so, follow these steps:

1 Select the cell or cells.

2 Choose the Format menu's Cells command. Excel displays the Format Cells dialog box.

3 Click the Border tab.

continues

Borders *(continued)*

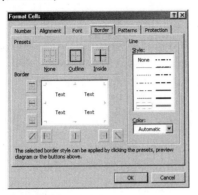

4 Select Border options to specify on which cell edges the border should appear. Click the preview diagram for each cell edge border, diagonal, or bisecting line you want. Or click the buttons around the preview diagram, or click the Presets buttons above the preview diagram.

5 Select Line Style options to specify border line thickness and other line style decisions—for example, choose dashes.

6 Select a border line color from the Line Color drop-down list box if you want something other than basic black.

SEE ALSO   **AutoFormatting Tables**

Calculating Formulas

Excel is very clever about the way it calculates **formulas.** Very clever indeed. It recognizes dependencies—so if one formula uses another formula's result, this other formula gets calculated first. Here's another clever twist. Unless you direct Excel to do otherwise, Excel recalculates your formulas whenever a formula or an input changes.

Three more points about recalculating: First, you won't always be able to tell when Excel recalculates formulas because it does so very quickly and in the background. Second, if Excel is still recalculating a worksheet or if it needs to recalculate a worksheet, the word *Calculate* appears on the status bar. Third, you can always press F9 to manually tell Excel to recalculate. You might do this, for example, if someone has told Excel not to automatically recalculate its formulas, which you can do by choosing the Tools menu's Options command and clicking its Calculation tab. To tell Excel not to automatically recalculate formulas, select the Manual option button on this tab.

Cell Address

A cell address identifies a specific cell by giving the cell's location using the column letter and row number. The cell address I81, for example, identifies the cell at the intersection of column I and row 81. U812 identifies the cell at the intersection of column U and row 812.

Cell addresses are handy because you can use them in **formulas.** When you use a cell address in a formula, Excel retrieves the value stored in the cell and uses this value in the formula.

If you want to refer to a cell on another **worksheet** in the **workbook,** you need to precede the cell address with the sheet name and an exclamation point. Sheet2!B52, for example, identifies the cell at the intersection of column B and row 52 on Sheet2 of the workbook.

If you want to refer to a cell in another workbook, you need to precede the cell address with the workbook name in brackets, the sheet name, and an exclamation point. [BUDGET.XLS]Sheet2!B52, for example, identifies the cell at the intersection of column B and row 52 on Sheet2 of the workbook named BUDGET.XLS.

Cell Protection

Adding cell protection to a workbook hides cell contents and prevents changes to the cell contents. Adding cell protection requires two actions. First you need to tell Excel which cells it should protect and how it should protect them. Then you need to tell Excel to turn on this protection.

Identifying Protected Cells

To tell Excel which cells it should protect and how it should protect them, follow these steps:

1 Select the cells.

2 Choose the Format menu's Cells command. Excel displays the Format Cells dialog box.

3 Click the Protection tab.

continues

Cell Protection *(continued)*

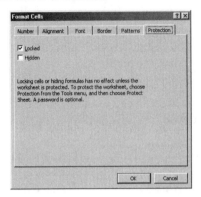

4 Select the Locked check box to prevent changes to cell contents.

5 Select the Hidden check box to prevent users from viewing cell contents on the formula bar. (The worksheet shows labels, values, and formula results, so do this to prevent users from viewing your formulas.)

6 Click OK.

7 Protect the worksheet as described in the next section, "Protecting a Worksheet."

Protecting a Worksheet

To turn on the protection in only the active worksheet, follow these steps:

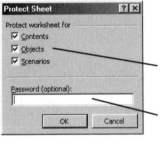

1 Choose the Tools menu's Protection command, and then choose the submenu's Protect Sheet command. Excel displays the Protect Sheet dialog box.

2 Select the Contents, Objects, or Scenarios check boxes to specify what you want to protect.

3 If you want, add a protection password.

Unprotecting a Worksheet

To turn off worksheet protection, choose the Tools menu's Protection command and then the submenu's Unprotect Sheet command. If you added a password, Excel will ask for the password before executing the command.

Protecting a Workbook

To turn on protection in all of a workbook's sheets, follow these steps:

1 Choose the Tools menu's Protection command, and then choose the submenu's Protect Workbook command. Excel displays the Protect Workbook dialog box.

2 Select the Structure or Windows check boxes to specify what you want to protect.

3 Optionally, add a protection password.

Unprotecting a Workbook

To turn off workbook protection, choose the Tools menu's Protection command and then choose the submenu's Unprotect Workbook command. If you added a password, Excel will ask for the protection password before executing the command.

SEE ALSO   Passwords; Scenarios

Cell Reference

Cell reference is simply another name for **cell address.** In other words, the cell reference is just another name for the column-letter-and-row-number combination that identifies the cell's location as the intersection of a worksheet column and row.

SEE ALSO   Active Cell

Cell Selector

The cell selector is the open rectangle, or box, that Excel uses to mark the **active cell.** If you're contused by this, start Excel and look at your screen. Now randomly press each of the direction keys several times. See the box that moves? That's the cell selector. The cell selector is also called a "cell pointer."

Changing Fonts

To change the **font** used for the selected cells' characters or the selected portion of text if you're editing a cell's contents, choose the Format menu's Cells command. In the Format Cells dialog box, click the Font tab.

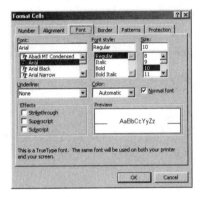

1 Select a font from the Font list box. Excel identifies printer fonts with the printer icon and identifies TrueType fonts with the ℡ logo.

2 Select a font style from the Font Style list box.

3 Select a point size from the Size list box. If you choose a larger point size, Excel will increase the row height accordingly. (Note that one point equals 1/72 inch.)

4 Optionally, select underlining from the Underline drop-down list box.

5 Select Effects check boxes to specify other character effects, such as subscript.

6 Select color from the Color drop-down list box. (Automatic means the Windows Control Panel controls color.)

7 Experiment with font changes, and then see their effects in the Preview box.

8 To return to the default, or suggested, font settings, select the Normal Font check box. When you do, Excel sets the Font to Arial, the Font Style to Regular, the Size to 10, and the Color to Automatic. Excel also removes underlining and any other special effects.

Another way to change the font

The toolbar provides tools for making some changes to the font used in the worksheet selection. The Font tool lets you change the font. The Font Size tool lets you adjust the font point size. The Bold, Italic and Underline tools let you boldface, italicize and underline the text. Note that if you don't see buttons for these tools on the toolbar, you can add them. For more information, refer to the **Adaptability** entry.

Chart

A chart is a picture that depicts worksheet data. In Excel, you create these pictures-worth-a-thousand-words with the **Chart Wizard.**

Adding gridlines to a chart SEE **Chart Gridlines**
Adding legends to a chart SEE **Chart Legends**
Adding titles to a chart SEE **Chart Titles**
Annotating charts with text SEE **Chart Text**
Changing chart colors SEE **Chart Colors**
Choosing a chart type SEE **Chart Types**
Creating a chart SEE **Chart Wizard**
Specifying how charts print SEE **Chart Page Setup**

Chart Colors

You can change the color of most parts of a chart if the chart is displayed on a separate sheet. If the chart isn't displayed on a separate sheet because it's an embedded chart, first select it by double-clicking.

Changing Chart Colors

To change the colors and fill effects in parts of a chart, follow these steps:

1 Double-click the part you want to change.

2 Click the Patterns tab.

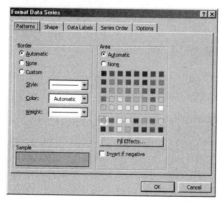

3 Select a color from the Border Color drop-down list box for the line drawn around the edge of the chart part—if the chart part has a border line.

4 Select a color from the Area option box for the chart part.

5 Click Fill Effects for any fill effects you want for the chart part.

continues

Chart Colors *(continued)*

Selecting a single data marker

To select a single **data marker** rather than all the data markers in the series, click the data marker twice and then double-click the selected data marker.

> **SEE ALSO   Editing Embedded Charts**

Chart Gridlines

You can use chart gridlines to make it easier to calibrate the values plotted in a chart and to differentiate the categories.

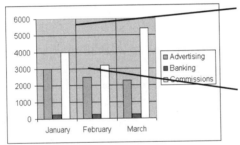

Category axis gridlines extend perpendicularly from the category axis, and help you keep the data categories straight.

Value axis gridlines extend perpendicularly from the value axis, and help you more easily calibrate plotted values.

Adding Value and Category Axis Gridlines

To add both value axis and category axis gridlines, follow these steps:

1 Choose the Chart menu's Chart Options command. Excel displays the Chart Options dialog box.

2 Click the Gridlines tab.

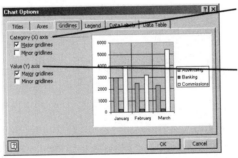

3 Select the Category (X) Axis check boxes to add or remove category axis gridlines.

4 Select the Value (Y) Axis check boxes to add or remove value axis gridlines.

Distinguishing between major and minor gridlines

Major gridlines extend from all the major tick marks. Minor gridlines extend from all the minor tick marks. Tick marks are those little lines, or dashes, that intersect the axes.

Chart Legends

You use chart legends to name the **data series** plotted in a chart. Assuming you were either lucky or astute enough to include the data series names in your chart data selection, you can add a chart legend by clicking the Chart toolbar's Legend button.

Unfortunately, if you don't include the data series names in your chart data selection, Excel doesn't know what to name the series. So it simply uses names such as Series1, Series2, and so on. For this reason, it's a good idea to include data series names in your chart data selection.

SEE ALSO   Chart Wizard; Data Categories

Chart Page Setup

Choose the File menu's Page Setup command and click the Chart tab to display the dialog box you use to specify how charts print. For this tab to appear, the active sheet must display a chart. If a chart is embedded, first select the chart.

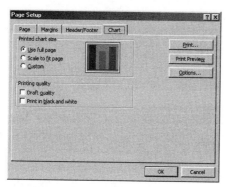

continues

Chart Page Setup *(continued)*

Changing Chart Size

To control chart size, click Printed Chart Size option buttons. Click Use Full Page if Excel should size the chart so that it uses the entire page. Click Scale To Fit Page if Excel should print the chart so that it's as large as will fit on the page but still use the same ratio of height to width as the chart on your screen. Click Custom if you want to print the chart using the on-screen dimensions.

Changing Print Quality

Select the Draft Quality check box if you want Excel to print faster but at a lower resolution. Select the Print In Black And White check box if you want Excel to print in black even though your printer outputs color.

SEE ALSO Printing

Chart Sheets

Excel charts appear either as objects embedded in a worksheet or as separate workbook sheets. When you click the **Chart Wizard** toolbar button or choose the Insert menu's Chart command to create a new chart, Excel gives you a choice. You can either embed a chart object in the active worksheet or you can place the chart on its own sheet by clicking the As New Sheet option button.

Chart Text

You can annotate charts by adding text. To add text to a chart, display the chart's sheet or select the embedded chart. Click the Drawing toolbar button to display the Drawing toolbar. On the Drawing toolbar, click the Text Box button. Click to establish one corner of the text box, and then drag until the box is the size you want. Type any text you want in the box, and it will wrap automatically. To start a new line, press Enter. Click outside the box when you're finished. You can move the text by selecting its box and dragging.

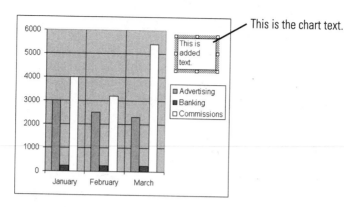

This is the chart text.

Formatting chart text

You can format chart text and **chart titles** in the same ways that you format cell contents. To format chart text, select the text and then choose the selected object from the Format menu. To format chart titles, select the title and then choose the Format menu's Selected Chart Title command.

Chart Titles

You can add text that names the chart and describes the axes. The easiest way to do this is to use the **Chart Wizard** when you create the chart. To modify an existing chart, first display the chart's sheet if it has its own sheet or select the chart if it's embedded. Next choose the Chart menu's Chart Options command, and click the Titles tab. Click the Chart Title box or one of the axis boxes, type the title text, and click OK.

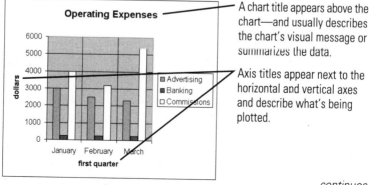

A chart title appears above the chart—and usually describes the chart's visual message or summarizes the data.

Axis titles appear next to the horizontal and vertical axes and describe what's being plotted.

continues

Chart Titles *(continued)*

Using different fonts in the same chart text

You can use different fonts in the same chart text. To format a title or text block differently, select a portion of the text and choose the Format menu's Selected Object or Selected Chart Title command. (The command name might be different, depending on what you select.)

Chart Types

Excel supplies 14 chart types and numerous subtypes. You can choose a chart type when you create the chart, and you can change the selected chart's type by choosing the Chart menu's Chart Type command. Which method you use depends on the visual comparison you want.

Type	What chart shows
	A *drawn area chart* plots data series as cumulative lines. The first data series values are plotted in a line. Then the second data series values are plotted in a line that gets stacked on top of the first line. Then the third data series values get stacked on top of the second line, and so on. Like its two-dimensional cousin, the *3-D area chart* plots data series with lines and then colors the area between the lines. Note that the 3-D area chart uses depth to organize the data series.
	A *bar chart* plots each data series' values by using horizontal bars. A *3-D bar chart* uses solid bars, and it is good for comparing individual values when the data category isn't time. A 3-D bar chart is a bit imprecise.
	A *column chart* is like a bar chart, but it plots each data series' values as vertical bars. A *3-D column chart* uses solid vertical bars. Note that some 3-D charts use depth to organize the data series. A column chart is good for comparing individual values when the data category is time. A 3-D column chart is a bit imprecise, too.
	A *line chart* plots each data series' values as points on a line. A *3-D line chart*, or ribbon chart, plots each data series' values as points on a ribbon, and it emphasizes trends in the data series values. A 3-D line chart is tricky to use.

Type	What chart shows
	A *pie chart* plots a single data series with each value in the series represented as a pie slice. A *3-D pie chart* represents data series values as pie wedges in a solid cylinder. It's probably the least effective chart type available because it's technically limited to a single data series and practically limited to a small number of values. (Otherwise the pie is sliced into too many pieces.) A 3-D pie chart is extremely difficult to use well because background wedges appear smaller than foreground wedges of the same value.
	A *doughnut chart* plots data series in rings, with each value in the series represented as a segment (bite) of the ring (doughnut).
	A *radar chart* plots data series values using a separate value axis for each category. The value axes radiate from the center of the chart.
	An *XY*, or *scatter, chart* uses two value axes gridlines to plot pairs of data points in a line. Because it visually shows the correlation between two data series, this is the most powerful and useful chart type available.
	A *surface chart* plots data series as lines in a two-dimensional grid and colors the areas between the lines. A *3-D surface chart* plots lines in a three-dimensional grid and colors the surfaces between the lines. A surface chart is useful for creating rectangular data maps. (A data map plots values on a map using latitudinal and longitudinal coordinates.)
	A *bubble chart* plots data series as circles of varying size in a two-dimensional grid. The larger the data value, the larger the circle.
	A *stock chart* plots daily stock prices for a series of stocks as vertical lines. A stock chart can show opening, closing, high, and low prices. In addition, a stock chart can plot daily trading volume as a bar chart.

continues

Chart Types *(continued)*

Type	What chart shows
	A *cylinder chart* is basically a bar or column chart that has cylindrically shaped bars or columns. Like bar and column charts, a cylinder chart is good for comparing individual values.
	A *cone chart* is basically a bar or column chart that has cone-shaped bars or columns. Like bar and column charts, a cone chart is good for comparing individual values.
	A *pyramid chart* is basically a bar or column chart that has pyramid-shaped bars or columns. Like bar and column charts, a pyramid chart is good for comparing individual values.

Chart Wizard

Excel's Chart Wizard creates charts that visually depict workbook data. To use the Chart Wizard, select the data you want to plot. In your selection, include the data series names. Be sure to include the category names too if they appear in the worksheet.

	A	B	C	D	E
1		January	February	March	Total
2	Advertising	3000	2500	2300	7800
3	Banking	250	250	250	750
4	Commissions	4000	3200	5400	12600
5	Total	7250	5950	7950	21150
6					

After you've selected the data you want to plot, click the Chart Wizard toolbar button. Excel displays the first Chart Wizard dialog box. To use the Chart Wizard, follow the on-screen instructions. Or refer to the **Office Assistant** for help in creating the chart. Note that if you want to accept the Chart Wizard's suggested settings for your chart, you can click Finish to instantly create the chart.

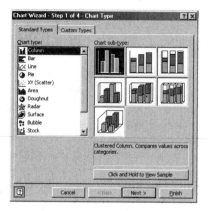

SEE ALSO   Environment: Microsoft Excel 2000 Charts

ClipArt Gallery SEE **Pictures**

Clipboard

When you copy or cut some selection from an Excel workbook, Excel copies your selection from the workbook to the Windows Clipboard, a temporary storage area. And when you later paste the selection, Excel copies the selection from the Clipboard to the workbook. If you copy or cut more than one selection to the Clipboard, Windows displays the Clipboard toolbar. It shows how many items you've stored on the clipboard. (If you don't see the Clipboard toolbar, choose the View menu's Toolbars command and then choose the submenu's Clipboard command.)

continues

Clipboard *(continued)*

If you choose the Edit menu's Paste command or click the Paste toolbar button, Excel (with Windows's help) inserts the most recent addition to the Clipboard. But you can use the Clipboard toolbar to copy some item other than the most recent Clipboard addition. To do this, click the picture representing the selection you want to copy. If you don't know which Clipboard picture represents what copied or cut selection, point to the picture so that Windows displays a pop-up box describing the Clipboard contents. Two more notes about the Clipboard toolbar: First, you can click the Paste All button to paste everything you've stored on the Clipboard into the active document—probably an Excel workbook. Second, you can click the Clipboard toolbar's Clear Clipboard button to erase the Clipboard.

SEE ALSO   Copying

Closing Workbooks

You close **workbooks** so that they don't consume memory and so that they don't clutter your screen.

Closing a Single Workbook

To close a workbook, click its Close button, which is the small button marked with an "X" located in the upper right corner of the window. You can also close a workbook if its window is active by choosing the File menu's Close command.

Closing All Workbooks

To close all the open workbook windows at once, hold down Shift and then choose the File menu's Close All command.

So you don't lose changes

If you've made changes to the workbook and haven't yet saved them, Excel asks whether you want to save before closing.

C

Collect And Copy

Collect And Copy refers to a new feature in Microsoft Office 2000 that lets you store more than one copied or cut selection on the Windows **Clipboard.**

Color

You can change the color of most parts of worksheets and charts.

Changing the color of border lines SEE **Borders**
Changing colors in a chart SEE **Chart Colors**
Changing the color of labels and values SEE **Fonts**
Changing cell background colors SEE **Patterns**

Coloring Worksheet Ranges

You can color a selected worksheet range by clicking the Fill Color toolbar button.

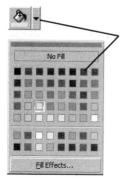

Click the down arrow next to the Fill Color button; then select one of the colors from the palette that Excel provides.

SEE ALSO   Coloring Worksheet Text; Formatting

Coloring Worksheet Text

You can color the characters in a selected worksheet range by clicking the Font Color toolbar button.

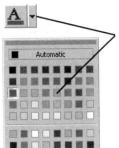

Click the down arrow next to the Font Color toolbar button; then select one of the colors from the palette that Excel provides.

SEE ALSO   **Coloring Worksheet Ranges; Formatting**

Columns

You can change the width of columns by using the mouse or choosing the Format menu's Column command and then choosing submenu commands. Using the mouse is easier. To change the width of a selected column or of several selected columns with the mouse, drag the edge of the column letter label.

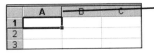

Drag the edge of the column letter label left or right to change a column's width. Excel changes the mouse pointer to a two-directional arrow when you position the mouse on the column edge.

SEE ALSO   **Rows**

Comments

You can use comments to document or describe the contents of a cell.

Adding and Editing Comments

To enter or edit a cell note, follow these steps:

1 Select the cell.

2 Choose the Insert menu's Comment command.

3 Type your comment in the box.

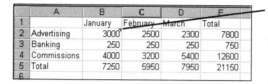

	A	B	C	D	E
1		January	F		Total
2	Advertising	3000	**steve:** This looks low to me.		7800
3	Banking	250			750
4	Commissions	4000			12600
5	Total	7250			21150
6					
7					

Locating Comments

To see a cell comment, move the mouse pointer over the cell.

	A	B	C	D	E
1		January	February	March	Total
2	Advertising	3000	2500	2300	7800
3	Banking	250	250	250	750
4	Commissions	4000	3200	5400	12600
5	Total	7250	5950	7950	21150
6					

To show you which cells have notes, Excel places a marker in the cell's upper right corner. Choose the View menu's Comments command to review all the comments on your worksheet.

Conditional Formatting

Conditional **formatting** is a special kind of cell formatting that changes the way cell entries look depending on their **values.** When you apply conditional formatting to a cell, you can set certain conditions that, if met, produce the formatting you choose. For example, you can use conditional formatting to highlight negative values by displaying them in red. Or you can make it easy to find all values in a certain range by formatting them in green or in italics. Or you can place a border around certain key terms. You get the idea.

To use conditional formatting, select a cell or a range of cells and choose the Format menu's Conditional Formatting command. When Excel displays the Conditional Formatting dialog box, follow the steps on the next page.

continues

Conditional Formatting *(continued)*

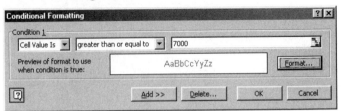

1 Specify whether you want the first condition to pertain to a value or a formula.

2 Tell Excel the logical operator to apply (for example, "between," "equal to," or "greater than").

3 Enter the value or values that the formatting depends upon. (They can be numbers or text.)

4 Click Add to add conditions.

5 Click Format to specify how you want the formatted value or values to look.

6 Click OK.

Conditional Functions

Conditional **functions** perform a logical test (described using **Boolean algebra**) and return a value or text string based on the results of the test.

Suppose, for example, that you're a teacher and you want a formula that compares a student's final test score, the value in the cell named TestScore, with 60. If the student's test score equals or exceeds this value, the student passes. If the student's test score is less than this value, the student fails. Here's an example of a conditional IF function:

=IF(TestScore>=60,"P", "F")

This IF function compares the value in the cell named TestScore with 60. If the value in TestScore equals or exceeds 60, the function returns the one-character string P. If the value in TestScore is less than 60, the function returns the one-character string F.

SEE ALSO   Argument

Converting Formulas into Numbers

If you want to convert the **formulas** in a worksheet range to **values,** follow these steps:

1 Select the range that contains the formulas you want to convert.

2 Choose the Edit menu's Copy command.

3 Choose the Edit menu's Paste Special command. Excel displays the Paste Special dialog box.

4 Select the Paste Values option button, and then click OK.

Copying

You can copy and paste **values, labels,** formats, worksheet selections, and even graphic objects. You can do so within Excel or between Excel and another Windows program.

Copying numeric formats SEE **Copying Cell Formats**
Copying values and labels SEE **Copying Data**
Copying worksheet formulas SEE **Copying Formulas**
Copying worksheet objects SEE **Copying Objects and Pictures**
Copying worksheet ranges SEE **Copying Ranges**

Copying Cell Formats

You can reuse the format of one cell for other cells.

Using the Format Painter Button

One way—and often the easiest way—to copy formats is with the Format Painter toolbar button. To do this, follow these steps:

1 Select a cell with the formatting that you want to reuse.

2 Click the Format Painter toolbar button.

3 Select the cells you want to format.

Copying Formats with Commands

You can also copy cell formats by choosing menu commands. To do this, follow the steps on the following page.

continues

Copying Cell Formats *(continued)*

1 Select the cell with the format you want to copy.

2 Choose the Edit menu's Copy command.

3 Select the cell or cells in which you want to use the format.

4 Choose the Edit menu's Paste Special command. Excel displays the Paste Special dialog box.

5 In the Paste section, click the Formats option button, and then click OK.

The Paste Special's Paste options let you control which features get pasted into other cells and reused.

The Paste Special's Operation options let you specify whether pasted values should be combined in some way with the values already in the cells. If you're pasting cell formats, operation options are disabled.

Copying Data

You can copy **values, labels,** and **formulas** between cells by using the mouse or menu commands.

Copying with the Mouse

To use the mouse, follow these steps:

1 Select the cell.

2 Hold down Ctrl, and drag the selected cell's border to its new location.

Copying with Commands

To use the Copy and Paste commands, follow these steps:

1 Select the cell with the value or the label.

2 Choose the Edit menu's Copy command.

3 Select the cell to which you want to copy the value or the label.

4 Choose the Edit menu's Paste command.

SEE ALSO **Clipboard; Copying Ranges; Drag-and-Drop; Fill Handle; Moving Data**

Copying Data Between Programs
SEE **Sharing Microsoft Excel Data**

Copying Formulas

You can copy formulas between cells. The way you do this, however, depends on whether you want Excel to adjust any **relative cell addresses** used in the formula.

When Excel Should Adjust Formulas

If you want Excel to adjust the formula's relative cell addresses, you can copy a formula the same way you copy values and labels. For example, you can select the cell with the formula, hold down Ctrl, and drag it. Or you can select the cell with the formula, choose the Edit menu's Copy command, select the cell to which you want to copy the formula, and choose the Edit menu's Paste command. Either way, Excel adjusts the formula's relative cell addresses.

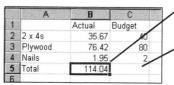

The formula =B2+B3+B4 adds the values in the cells above it.

Rather than reenter the same basic formula into cell C5, you can copy the formula in cell B5 to cell C5. Because the formula in B5 uses relative cell addresses, Excel pastes the formula =C2+C3+C4 into cell C5.

When Excel Shouldn't Adjust Formulas

If you don't want Excel to adjust the relative cell addresses used in the formula, you can make these relative cell addresses absolute (by editing the formula), or you can follow these steps:

1 Select the cell with the formula.

2 Click the **formula bar,** and then select the formula (in the formula bar).

3 Choose the Edit menu's Copy command, or click the Copy toolbar button.

4 Press Esc, or click the formula bar's Cancel button.

5 Select the cell to which you want to copy the formula.

6 Choose the Edit menu's Paste command, or click the Paste toolbar button.

SEE ALSO Absolute Cell Address; Copying Data; Moving Data

Copying Objects and Pictures

To copy worksheet objects and pictures you've inserted, follow these steps:

1 Select the object or picture. Excel adds selection handles.

2 Hold down Ctrl.

3 Drag the picture to another location. (As you start to drag, Excel creates a new copy of the object or picture.)

SEE ALSO **Moving Objects and Pictures; Resizing Pictures; Worksheet Pictures**

Copying Ranges

You can use either the Copy and Paste menu commands or the mouse to copy a range.

Copying with the Mouse

To copy a worksheet range (and the **labels, values,** and **formulas** it holds) with the mouse, follow these steps:

1 Select the cells you want to copy.

2 Hold down Ctrl.

3 Click the edge of the range.

4 Drag the selected range to the new location.

Copying with Commands

To copy a worksheet range with the Copy and Paste commands or the equivalent tools, follow these steps:

1 Select the cells you want to copy by dragging the mouse between the opposite corners of the worksheet range. Excel highlights the range to indicate it's been selected.

2 Choose the Edit menu's Copy command, or click the Copy toolbar button.

3 Select the cell in the upper left corner of the range into which the copied cells should be placed.

4 Choose the Edit menu's Paste command, or click the Paste toolbar button.

Automatic formula adjustments

When you copy a worksheet range, Excel adjusts the **relative cell addresses** used by any of the copied formulas.

SEE ALSO **Clipboard; Copying Data; Copying Formulas; Fill Handle; Moving Data**

Copying Sheets SEE Moving and Copying Sheets

Creating Lists

To create a list on a worksheet, follow these steps:

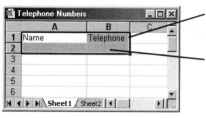

1 Enter the column headers, or field names, in the first worksheet row.

2 Select the header row, and the next empty row.

3 Choose the Data menu's Form command. Excel might display a dialog box that says it can't detect the headers. Click OK if you get this message. Excel displays a data entry form for filling the list.

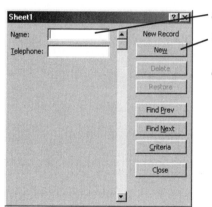

4 Fill in the text boxes.

5 Click New to add an entry to the list.

6 Repeat steps 4 and 5 for every entry you want to add to the list.

SEE ALSO   **Environment: List Management; Naming Sheets**

Currency Symbols

Excel uses a currency symbol to punctuate monetary values that you format as currency. Which currency symbol Excel uses depends on the Control Panel's Regional Settings.

continues

Currency Symbols *(continued)*

Changing Currency Symbols

To change the currency symbol Excel uses, click the Start button and then choose Settings and Control Panel. Double-click the Regional Settings icon, click the Currency tab, and then enter a new currency symbol in the Currency symbol text box.

If you don't see the currency symbol you want to use on the keyboard, you'll need to enter the ANSI character code for the symbol. You do this by holding down the Alt key and using the numeric keypad to type the ANSI character code for the symbol. For example, hold down Alt and type 157 to enter the Japanese Yen symbol (¥). Hold down Alt and type 156 to enter the British Pounds Sterling symbol (£). (For other ANSI character codes, use Windows' Character Map program.)

About Control Panel changes

Some Control Panel changes won't take effect until the next time you start Windows. To make your Control Panel changes take effect, close your applications and restart Windows.

SEE ALSO   Formatting Numbers; Unicode

Custom Filtering

The Data menu's Filter command displays a submenu that provides two methods for **filtering lists:** AutoFilter and Advanced Filter. The quicker and easier method is to use the AutoFilter command. To use AutoFilter, select the entire list, including both the header row and all the entry rows. Choose the Data menu's Filter command, and then choose the submenu's AutoFilter command. When you do this, Excel turns the cells in the header row into drop-down list boxes. To filter your list, select an entry from one of these list boxes.

Databases SEE List Management

Data Categories

Data categories organize the values in a chart's **data series.** This sounds confusing, but let me give you an easy rule of thumb. In any chart that shows how some value changes over time, data categories are time periods. So in a chart that plots sales over a five-year period—say, 2001 to 2005—it's the years that are the data categories.

Data Markers

Data markers are the visual building blocks that Excel uses to draw a chart. Each Excel **chart type** uses a different data marker. A column chart, for example, has column data markers. A pie chart has pie-slice data markers. A line chart uses points along a line, and so on. Interestingly, by the way, Excel also lets you use pictures as data markers.

SEE ALSO   Picture Charts

Data Series

A data series is simply a set of related values plotted with the same **data marker** in an Excel chart. If you find the term *data series* confusing, you can usually identify the data series that a chart plots by asking yourself, "What am I plotting?" Every one-word answer will identify a data series. For example, if you ask the "What am I plotting?" question about a chart that plots sales revenue over five years, you can answer, "Sales." Sales, then, is a data series. By the way, the data markers that visually represent the set of sales values will all look similar. For example, the sales data series might be depicted with a set of red bars or as points along the same line.

SEE ALSO   Data Categories

Data Validation SEE Auditing Worksheets

Date and Time Functions

Excel provides more than a dozen functions to make working with **date values** and **time values** easier. Using the DATE function, for example, you can easily determine the date value for a particular day. The function below returns the date value for December 31, 2001, which is 37256, by using as function arguments the year number (2001), the month number (12), and the day number (31):

    =DATE(2001,12,31)

SEE ALSO   Argument; Function

Date Formats

Excel provides 15 date formats that you can use to make **date values** understandable. To format a date, select the cell or range with the date values. Then choose the Format menu's Cells command, and select Date from the Category list box. Finally, select one of the date formats from the Type list box.

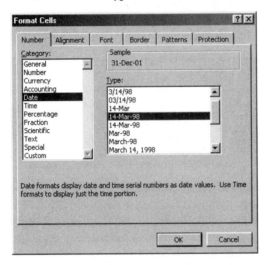

SEE ALSO   **Formatting Numbers; Time Values**

Date Values

Excel lets you use values to represent dates: 1 to represent January 1, 1900; 2 to represent January 2, 1900; and so on, through 2,958,465 to represent December 31, 9999. And to make these sorts of values meaningful, Excel formats date values to look like dates.

Date values allow you to perform date-based arithmetic, which is often very handy. Say you've got a workbook that keeps a record of invoices and estimates payment dates. If an invoice is due 30 days from the invoice date—for example, October 28, 2001—you can calculate the invoice due date by adding the value 30 to the date value for October 28, 2001 (37192). The formula result, 37222, gives the day you should expect payment. Of course, 37222 isn't very meaningful, but once you tell Excel to format this as November 27, 2001, things begin to look pretty clear.

Moving worksheets to the Apple Macintosh

If you move Excel workbooks between Windows and the **Apple Macintosh,** be forewarned: Excel for the Macintosh uses a different date value numbering scheme. On the Macintosh, the value 1 represents January 2, 1904. (If you want Excel for Windows to use the same date value numbering scheme as Excel for the Macintosh, choose the Tools menu's Options command, click the Calculation tab, and select the 1904 Date System check box.)

SEE ALSO   **Date Formats; Formulas; Time Values**

Default File Location

If you want Excel to suggest a default location for the workbooks you save, follow these steps:

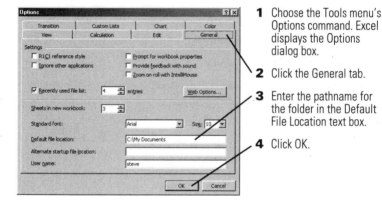

1 Choose the Tools menu's Options command. Excel displays the Options dialog box.

2 Click the General tab.

3 Enter the pathname for the folder in the Default File Location text box.

4 Click OK.

SEE ALSO   **Saving Workbooks**

Default Fonts

Excel, by default, uses 10-**point** Arial type for worksheets. To use another **font,** follow these steps:

1 Choose the Tools menu's Options command. Excel displays the Options dialog box.

2 Click the General tab.

continues

Default Fonts *(continued)*

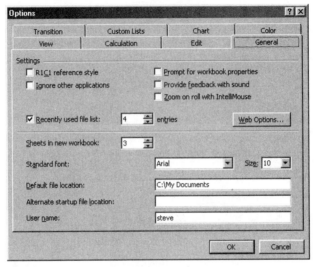

3 Select a font from the Standard Font drop-down list box.

4 Select a point size from the Size drop-down list box.

5 Click OK. Restart Excel to have your font and size settings appear in worksheets.

Default Workbooks

You can tell Excel that it should open a particular workbook every single time you start Excel. To do this, simply save the workbook in the XLStart folder. You'll find the XLStart folder in one of the Microsoft Office folders, which you'll find in the Program Files folder.

SEE ALSO   Saving Workbooks

Deleting

You can remove—or delete—cells, charts, columns, rows, and worksheets.

Removing cells SEE **Deleting Cells**
Removing charts SEE **Deleting Sheets**
Removing columns SEE **Deleting Columns and Rows**
Removing rows SEE **Deleting Columns and Rows**
Removing worksheets SEE **Deleting Sheets**

Deleting vs. erasing

When you delete a cell, column, or row, it no longer exists in the worksheet. In other words, Excel removes the entire cell, column, or row, and then rearranges the worksheet so that there are no holes, or gaps. In comparison, when you clear, or erase, a cell, column, or row, Excel removes only the cell's contents and formatting.

Deleting Cells

To delete, or remove, cells from a row or a column, select the cells and then choose the Edit menu's Delete command.

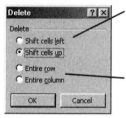

Select a Delete option to tell Excel how it should fill the "hole" left after the deletion. Click Shift Cells Up to move up the cells beneath the selected cells, or click Shift Cells Left to move to the left the cells to the right of the selected cells.

Don't click the Entire Row or Entire Column option buttons unless you want to delete the selected cells' rows or columns.

SEE ALSO   Deleting Columns and Rows

Deleting Columns and Rows

To delete columns or rows from a worksheet, select the columns or rows and then choose the Edit menu's Delete command.

SEE ALSO   Deleting Cells; Editing Cell Contents; Error Messages

Deleting List Entries SEE **Editing Lists**

Deleting Sheets

To delete a **worksheet** or a **chart sheet,** display the sheet and then choose the Edit menu's Delete Sheet command.

Delimited Text Files

A delimited text file is a file that uses a standard character—for example, the Tab character—to break apart the lines, or rows, of information. You can import text files, including delimited text files, into Excel by choosing the File menu's Open command. When you attempt to open a delimited text file, Excel starts a wizard that helps you import the file's information.

SEE ALSO   ASCII Text Files; Importing Text Files

Dependents

A dependent is a cell with a formula that references, or addresses, other cells. For example, if cell A1 uses the formula =B12+E6, it uses the values in cells B12 and E6. Cell A1, then, is a dependent cell, because it "depends on" cells B12 and E6.

SEE ALSO   Auditing Worksheets; Precedents

Desktop

The desktop is what you see when you start Windows. It's the desktop, for example, that provides shortcut icons and on which the Start button and Taskbar rest. This desktop doesn't directly have anything to do with Excel—except that both the Open and Save dialog boxes let you easily store and retrieve Excel workbooks from there.

Detect And Repair

Microsoft Office programs provide a Detect And Repair command on their Help menus. You can choose this command to direct an Office program, such as Excel, to look for and if possible repair problems with noncritical files. Note that Excel automatically identifies and repairs problems with critical files.

Drag-and-Drop

Drag-and-drop is a technique that lets you move and copy pieces of a **workbook** with the mouse.

Moving with Drag-and-Drop

To move some piece of a workbook—such as a cell, a range, or a picture—select it and then drag it to its new location.

Copying with Drag-and-Drop

To copy some piece of a workbook—such as a cell, a range, or a picture—select it, press Ctrl, and then drag it to its new location.

Drag-and-drop trick

If you click a cell or range using the mouse's right button (instead of the left button), Excel displays a **shortcut menu** of commands you can use to copy or move the selection in different ways.

SEE ALSO   Clipboard; Copying; Fill Handle; Moving Data

Drawing

Click the Drawing button, which appears on Excel's Standard toolbar, to draw objects such as arrows, circles, and rectangles by dragging the mouse. Clicking the Drawing toolbar button activates the Drawing toolbar shown below.

Click the down arrows on the Drawing toolbar to display palettes of lines, shapes, text effects, and colors.

Click to select a drawing tool from a palette. Then click where you want to start drawing, hold down the mouse button, and drag to draw whatever shows on the tool's face.

Click the Draw button to display a menu of drawing-related commands.

SEE ALSO   Moving Objects and Pictures; Pictures

Editing Cell Contents

To change the formula, value, or text stored in a cell, replace the cell's contents by entering some new formula, value, or piece of text into the cell. You can also double-click the cell so that Excel turns the cell into an editable text box. Now make your changes.

You can also use the formula bar to edit the **active cell.** Simply click the formula bar, and Excel adds two buttons related to editing in the formula bar.

The formula bar shows the contents of the selected cell—in this case, a simple formula. It works like an editable text box.

When you finish, click the Enter button.

If you don't want to move the edited contents shown on the formula bar to the cell, click the Cancel button.

Editing Embedded Charts

If you want to edit an embedded chart, select it. Use the buttons on the Chart toolbar to make additions and changes. When you finish editing the chart, press Esc or select a worksheet cell to redisplay the regular worksheet menu bar.

SEE ALSO   Chart Colors; Chart Wizard

Editing Lists

To edit a list, select the list (including the column headings) and then choose the Data menu's Form command. To make changes in the Data Form dialog box, follow these steps:

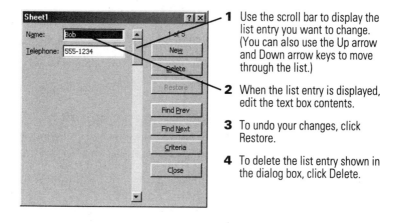

1 Use the scroll bar to display the list entry you want to change. (You can also use the Up arrow and Down arrow keys to move through the list.)

2 When the list entry is displayed, edit the text box contents.

3 To undo your changes, click Restore.

4 To delete the list entry shown in the dialog box, click Delete.

More about Restore

To reverse editing changes you've made to the list entry currently displayed, click Restore. Note, though, that you must click Restore before displaying another list entry. Also, Restore won't restore a list entry you've previously deleted.

SEE ALSO   Creating Lists; List Management; Searching Lists

E-Mail

You may be able to e-mail the active Excel workbook to someone else by choosing the File menu's Send To command and then choosing the submenu's Mail Recipient (As Attachment) command. When you choose this command, Windows starts your e-mail program and attaches the active workbook to the message. To complete the message, supply the recipient's e-mail name and click the Send toolbar button. Note that Excel doesn't provide this command unless it knows you have e-mail service.

Embedding and Linking Existing Objects

To create an object using an existing file, follow these steps:

1 Choose the Insert menu's Object command. Excel displays the Object dialog box.

2 Click the Create From File tab.

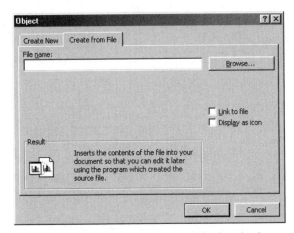

3 If necessary, click Browse to open a dialog box that lets you search your computer's disks and folders for the file you want.

4 Identify the object file in the File Name list box.

5 Select the Link To File check box if you want Windows to update the object for subsequent file changes.

6 Select the Display As Icon check box if you want Excel to display an icon to represent the objects.

7 Click OK when you finish describing the embedded or linked object. Excel links or embeds the object into your Excel workbook.

SEE ALSO **Copying Objects and Pictures; Moving Objects and Pictures; Pictures; Resizing Pictures**

Embedding New Objects

To create an object from scratch using an application other than Excel, follow these steps:

1 Choose the Insert menu's Object command. Excel displays the Object dialog box.

2 Click the Create New tab.

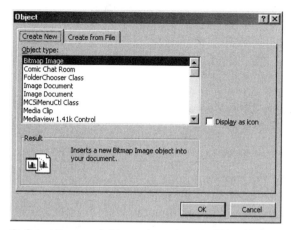

3 Select the type of object to insert from the Object Type list box.

4 Select the Display As Icon check box to see the embedded object as an icon rather than the full embedded object.

5 When you click OK, Excel starts the appropriate application so that you can create the object. (To see the object in your Excel worksheet, click outside the object on the worksheet.)

SEE ALSO **Embedding and Linking Existing Objects**

Entering Data

To enter a value or a piece of text in a cell, simply click the cell and then type whatever you want stored in the cell. You can enter **values**, **labels** (pieces of text), or **formulas** in this way. You can enter labels as long as 255 characters. You can enter values as long as 15 digits.

Predictable patterns

If you want to enter values that follow a predictable pattern, choose the Edit menu's Fill command and then choose the submenu's Series command. What's a predictable pattern? Good question. Here are a couple of examples: a series of month-end date values or a set of numbers that increase by a set value (such as 1) or by a set percentage (such as 5 percent).

SEE ALSO **Fill Handle; Scientific Notation**

Erasing Cells

You can erase cell contents, **formatting,** comments, and hyperlinks by choosing the Edit menu's Clear command and then choosing submenu commands.

Erasing a Cell's Contents

To erase cell contents (meaning the stuff—values, labels, or formulas—stored in the cell), choose Contents Del or press Delete.

Erasing Formatting

To erase cell formatting, choose Formats.

Erasing Cell Comments

To erase cell comments, choose Comments.

Erasing Hyperlinks

To delete a hyperlink from a cell, choose Hyperlinks.

Erasing It All

If you want to wipe out everything associated with the cell—its contents, its formats, its **comments,** and its hyperlinks—choose All.

The wrong way to erase

Don't remove a cell's contents with the Spacebar. When you select a cell and then press the Spacebar, you don't erase the cell's contents. Instead you replace the cell contents with a space character.

SEE ALSO **Deleting; Deleting Cells**

Erasing Workbooks

Workbooks are files stored on disk. To erase them, therefore, choose the File menu's Delete command in Windows Explorer or My Computer. For information about how to use Windows Explorer or My Computer to erase a workbook file, refer to the Help that came with your copy of Windows.

If you accidentally erase a workbook

You should know that it may be possible to recover, or unerase, a workbook file. If you've only recently deleted a file, you can retrieve it by opening the Recycle Bin and dragging the file to another folder.

Error Messages

If a **formula** doesn't work right and Excel knows why, Excel will display one of the following error messages:

Message	The problem is that your formula
#DIV/0	Attempts the undefined operation of dividing by zero.
#N/A	Addresses a cell that holds the "not available" code, #N/A.
#NAME?	Uses a cell name you haven't defined or one you've misspelled.
#NULL	Tries to return a value that doesn't exist.
#NUM!	Attempts some impossible mathematical operation such as calculating the root of a negative value.
#REF!	Addresses a cell or a range that doesn't exist—perhaps because you deleted it.
#VALUE!	Tries to arithmetically manipulate something that's not a value—such as text.

SEE ALSO   Auditing Worksheets

Exiting Excel

To exit Excel—or just about any other Windows-based program—choose the File menu's Exit command. Or you can close the Excel program window—for example, by clicking its Close button. Excel will ask if you want to save workbooks with unsaved changes.

SEE ALSO   Closing Workbooks; Saving Workbooks

Exporting

Exporting is copying a workbook so that you or someone else can use it with another spreadsheet or word-processor program. You can export an Excel workbook by saving it in a file format that the other program can use.

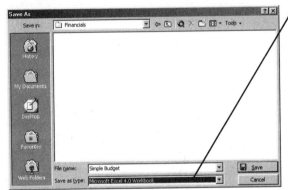

To specify another file format, select it from the Save As Type drop-down list box when you save the workbook.

Favorites

Windows will maintain a list of your favorite web pages. Although you create this list of favorites with Windows or Microsoft Internet Explorer, the favorites list is relevant to Excel. Both the Open dialog box and the Save dialog box provide a Favorites shortcut icon, which you can click to display your favorites list.

Filenames

You give a workbook its filename when you choose the File menu's Save As command.

Choosing a Filename

Windows file-naming rules apply to Excel workbook files. A filename can have as many as 256 characters. All numbers and letters that appear on your keyboard are okay. And so are many other characters. You can't, however, use characters that Windows expects to be used in special ways, such as slashes, asterisks, and question marks. If you need more information about this, refer to Windows Help.

Choosing a File Extension

The Windows file extension, by the way, isn't something you need to worry about. Windows and Excel supply and use file extensions to identify file types. You can accept the default Excel workbook file type, XLS, or you can select some other file type from the File Save dialog box's File Type drop-down list box.

SEE ALSO Save Options; Saving Workbooks

File Properties

In addition to the worksheets and charts you store in a workbook, you can store additional information that describes the workbook itself and makes it easier to find. You collect and store this additional information by filling out the Summary tab of the workbook Properties dialog box, which Excel displays when you choose the File menu's Properties command. For example, you can enter a title for your workbook. And you can add keywords that will make it easy to later find the workbook file using the Find command on the Tools drop-down menu in the Open dialog box.

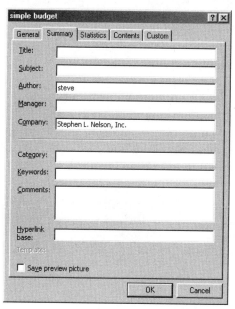

Fill Handle

By dragging a fill handle with the mouse, you can fill a selected range with **formulas, values,** or **labels.** You can also duplicate a pattern or a series if Excel can determine what the pattern or series is. The easiest and most expeditious way for you to become comfortable with the fill handle's operation is just to experiment with it. For example, enter a value, label, or formula into a cell. And then drag the cell's fill handle up, down, left, right, and so on. You'll quickly see how the fill handle works.

	A	B	C	D	E
1		January	February	March	Total
2	Advertising	3000	2500	2300	7800
3	Banking	250	250	250	750
4	Commissions	4000	3200	5400	12600
5	Total	7250	5950	7950	21150
6					
7					

This is the fill handle you drag.

A fill handle trick

If you drag a selection's fill handle using the right mouse button, Excel displays a **shortcut menu** of commands you can use to specify exactly what and how Excel should fill as soon as you release the right mouse button.

SEE ALSO Filling Cells

Filling Cells

To fill a selected range with **formulas, values,** or **labels,** use the **fill handle,** as described above, or choose the Edit menu's Fill command and then choose one of the submenu's commands, as described below:

Command	What it does
Down	Copies contents of the topmost row into rows below.
Right	Copies contents of the leftmost column into columns to the right.
Up	Copies contents of the bottommost row into rows above.

Command	What it does
Left	Copies contents of the rightmost column into columns to the left.
Across Worksheets	Copies contents of the first workbook sheet into second and subsequent worksheets.
Series	Fills cells with a series of values that fit a predictable pattern.
Justify	Rearranges the active cell's label so that it evenly fills the selected cells.

SEE ALSO   Fill Series

Fill Series

Sometimes you'll want to fill cells with a series of **values** that fit a predictable pattern: only even numbers, for example, or month-end dates. Excel provides a special Fill submenu command, Series, which lets you do just this. To use the Series command, follow these steps:

1 Enter enough of the series' values to establish the pattern.

2 Select the cells with the values and those you want to fill.

3 Choose the Edit menu's Fill command, and then choose the submenu's Series command. Excel displays the Series dialog box.

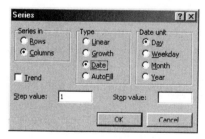

4 Indicate whether the series should be filled a row at a time or a column at a time.

5 Describe the pattern type.

continues

Fill Series *(continued)*

Pattern	Description
Linear	Create the pattern by adding the step value to the preceding cell's value.
Growth	Create the pattern by multiplying the step value by the preceding cell's value.
Date	Create a date-based pattern as described by the Step Value and Date Unit option.
AutoFill	Create a pattern based on the first cell's value. (AutoFill copies formulas, and it linearly adjusts values by the step value.)

6 Enter the step value used to create the pattern.

7 Optionally, enter the stop value that terminates the pattern.

A fill series trick

You can drag a **fill handle** to fill cells with a series of values or labels, too. For example, if you drag the fill handle of a cell containing the label January, Excel fills the next cells with the labels February, March, April, and so on. For Excel to determine the series pattern, however, you may need to select a range of cells (so Excel knows the step value). This process is called "autofilling."

SEE ALSO   Filling Cells

Filtering Lists

When you filter a list, you actually create a new list of entries that match a specified description.

Filtering an Existing List

1 Select the list.

	A	B	C
1	Name	State	Sales
2	Bob	Washington	120000
3	Jim	California	145000
4	Jeff	Oregon	35000
5	Gwen	Idaho	89000
6	Yuri	Montana	102000
7			

2 Choose the Data menu's Filter command, and then choose the submenu's AutoFilter command. Excel turns the header, or column heading, cells into drop-down list boxes.

	A	B	C
1	Name ▾	State ▾	Sales ▾

3 Describe the list entries you want on your new list by activating the header, or column heading, drop-down list boxes and selecting a value. Or select one of the other entries, such as All, Blanks, NonBlanks, or Custom.

4 If you select Custom, Excel displays the Custom AutoFilter dialog box.

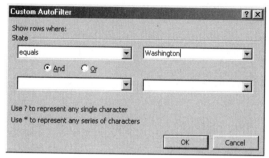

5 Select operators and values from the drop-down list boxes to create a **Boolean algebra** expression that describes the filter; for example, selecting *equals* from the first list box and *Washington* from the second list box tells Excel you want list entries that show the state as Washington.

Filtering with wildcards

When you enter **values,** you can use the question mark (?) character to represent any single character. And you can use the asterisk (*) character to represent any group of characters. The filter *Name equals B??* would return any three-character name starting with the letter B. The filter *State equals W** would return any state name starting with the letter W.

6 Create compound AND/OR filters by selecting the AND/OR options and using the second, lower set of operator and value drop-down list boxes.

7 After you specify the filter, click OK. Excel creates a new list of only those entries that match the filter.

Creating a New List from a Filtered List

To create a new list using the filtered list, copy the filtered list to a new worksheet location.

Displaying an Entire List Again

To display the entire list again, choose the Data menu's Filter command and then choose the submenu's Show All command. Choosing this command, in effect, unfilters a previously filtered list.

continues

Filtering Lists *(continued)*

Removing the AutoFilter Drop-Down List Boxes

To remove the AutoFilter drop-down list boxes, choose the Data menu's Filter command and then choose the submenu's AutoFilter command. The AutoFilter command is really a toggle switch, so choosing the command a second time turns off the AutoFilter feature.

Using Advanced Filters

The Filter submenu's Advanced Filter command displays a dialog box you use to identify the worksheet ranges holding the list and the filter descriptions (which need to be in the form of **Boolean algebra** expressions). Most people shouldn't ever need to use the Advanced Filter command.

SEE ALSO   **Creating Lists; Sorting Lists**

Financial Functions

Excel provides 52 financial functions for making depreciation expense calculations, for performing standard investment calculations such as the internal rate of return, and for calculating loan variables such as the periodic payment. For example, to calculate the monthly payment on a $10,000 loan with 60 months, or periods, of payments and a 1 percent per month interest rate, you can use the loan payment function shown below:

=PMT(.01,60,1000)

SEE ALSO   **Argument; Function; Troubleshooting: A Financial Function Doesn't Work Correctly**

Finding Cells

Choose the Edit menu's Find command to locate cells with specified contents: a fragment of text, part of a formula, a cell name or address, or a value.

Using the Find Command

To use the Find command, select the worksheet range Excel should search and then choose the command from the Edit menu. If Excel finds a cell, it makes that cell active.

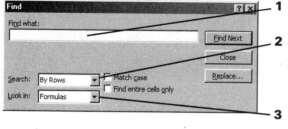

1 Specify what you're looking for.

2 Indicate whether Excel should search column by column or row by row.

3 Indicate where Excel should look: in formulas, at values, or in cell notes.

4 Click Find Next to start and restart the search.

Considering Case in a Search

Select the Match Case and Find Entire Cells Only check boxes to indicate whether Excel should consider case (lower vs. upper) in its search and look for entire cells rather than portions of cells.

SEE ALSO   Replacing Cell Contents; Searching Lists

Finding Files

You can use the Files Or Folders command on the Find submenu of the Windows Start menu to locate workbooks based on characteristics of the file and summary information collected about the file. For step-by-step information on how to use this command to find a lost workbook, refer to **Troubleshooting: You Can't Find a File.**

Fonts

You can use a wide variety of fonts in your worksheets. With fonts, you can even include Greek symbols and other special characters. Here are a few examples:

Clean and attractive, **Arial** resembles Helvetica.

`Courier New` looks like typewriter output.

Times New Roman uses serifs—little cross-strokes—to make characters easier to read.

SEE ALSO   Changing Fonts

Footers

Page footers can be added to the bottom of printed worksheets and charts.

SEE ALSO   Headers and Footers

Formatting

You can add formatting to cells to control value punctuation, alignment of values and labels, font styles and point sizes, border lines, and background cell patterns. You can also add a special type of formatting, called **cell protection,** that prevents changes to cell contents and that hides cell formulas.

Adding background shading SEE **Patterns**
Adding border lines SEE **Borders**
Alignment of values and labels in cells SEE **Aligning Labels and Values**
Changing font styles and point sizes SEE **Fonts**
Formatting date values SEE **Date Formats**
Formatting time values SEE **Time Formats**
Preventing cell changes and hiding cell formulas SEE **Cell Protection**
Using (and reusing) formatting combinations SEE **Styles**
Value punctuation, including currency symbols and commas SEE **Formatting Numbers**

Formatting Numbers

You can add formatting to **values** in two ways: by including the formatting when you enter the value and by choosing the Format menu's Cells command.

Formatting During Data Entry

Often it's easiest to include the formatting when you enter a value into the cell. This cell shown below, for example, holds the value 12345.67. But because I entered $12,345.67 into the cell, Excel formats the cell so that the displayed value shows a dollar sign and a comma.

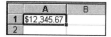

Formatting with the Format Cells Command

You can also format numbers in selected cells by choosing the Format menu's Cells command and then clicking the Number tab.

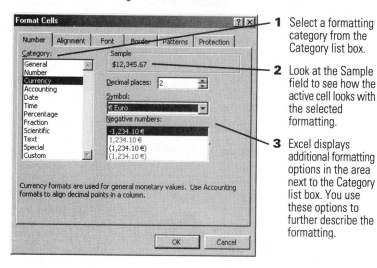

1 Select a formatting category from the Category list box.

2 Look at the Sample field to see how the active cell looks with the selected formatting.

3 Excel displays additional formatting options in the area next to the Category list box. You use these options to further describe the formatting.

SEE ALSO Scientific Notation

Formula Bar

The formula bar is that space under the toolbar.

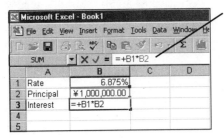

When you enter labels, values, and formulas into worksheet cells, Excel displays what you enter in the formula bar. If you select a cell by clicking, Excel also uses the formula bar to display the cell's contents. And if you click the formula bar, Excel lets you edit the cell's contents using the formula bar.

SEE ALSO   Editing Cell Contents

Formulas

In Excel, you use formulas to calculate **values.** To build a formula, select the cell in which the formula should go, type the equal sign (=) to indicate that what you're about to type is a formula, and type the formula using standard arithmetic operators, values, **cell addresses,** and even cell names. The table that follows shows some sample Excel formulas:

Formula	What happens
=2+2	Adds 2 and 2, returning the not-surprising result of 4.
=24.5-12	Subtracts 12 from 24.5.
=I81/U812	Divides the value in cell I81 by the value in cell U812.
=RATE*PRINCIPAL	Multiplies the values in the cells named RATE and PRINCIPAL.
=1000^2	Squares the value 1000.

Excel applies the standard rules of operator precedence in a formula that uses more than one operator: exponential operations are performed first, then division and multiplication, and then addition and subtraction. But you can override these standard rules by using parentheses. Excel will first perform operations inside parentheses.

The table that follows shows two more examples of simple formulas. Both use the same values and operators, but they return different results because of the way parentheses change the order of the arithmetic operations.

Formula	Result
=1+2*3	7
= (1+2)*3	9

Selective formulas

If you want to count the times a particular value or label occurs in a range of cells, or if you want to tally a value for some subset of the entries in a list (or if you want to do something that sounds like either of these tasks), choose the Data menu's Filter and Subtotals commands. Together, they'll make these selective calculations easy and straightforward.

SEE ALSO   Filtering Lists; Function; Functions; Subtotaling Lists

Fractions

To enter a fraction in a cell, type the equals sign and then the fraction. In other words, enter a formula for the fraction. For example, to enter the fraction 1/4, type =1/4. Excel stores the equivalent decimal value for the fraction.

SEE ALSO   Formulas

Full Screen

You can use almost all of your screen to display a workbook's sheets. When you view a workbook in a full screen, Excel displays only the menu bar and the workbook. Excel doesn't display the toolbars, the application window's title bar, and the document window's title bar.

continues

Full Screen *(continued)*

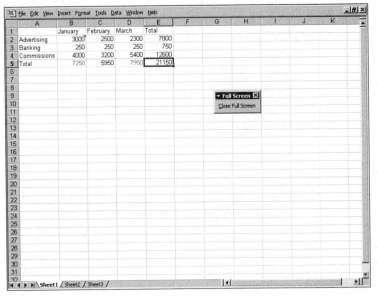

To view the Excel application window as a full screen, choose the View menu's Full Screen command. To return to the regular view of the application window, choose the View menu's Full Screen command again. Or click the Full Screen toolbar button.

Function

The Function command enters functions into cells, and it also lets you use **functions** to quickly perform complicated calculations.

To use the Function command, follow these steps:

1 Choose the Insert menu's Function command, or click the Function toolbar button. Excel displays the first Paste Function dialog box.

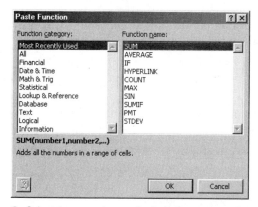

2 Select the general type of calculation you want from the Function Category list box. Excel displays a list of the functions in that category.

3 Select the calculation you want from the Function Name list.

4 Click OK to move to the second dialog box.

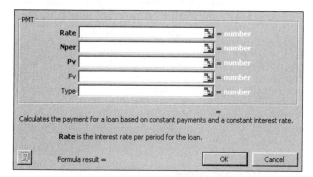

5 Enter the function arguments as values, cell addresses, or cell names in the text boxes. Excel displays the function value to the right of the text box. (Required argument names appear in **bold**; optional argument names don't.)

6 To place the function into the active cell, click OK. (If you don't want to place the function into the active cell, click Cancel.)

SEE ALSO Formulas

Functions

Functions are prefabricated **formulas** you can use to make worksheet construction easier—and more accurate. In a function, you name the formula to be calculated and supply the inputs, or **arguments.**

continues

Functions *(continued)*

Conditional test or logical formulas SEE **Conditional Functions**
Date and time value formulas SEE **Date and Time Functions**
Depreciation, investment, and loan formulas SEE **Financial Functions**
Logarithmic, mathematical, trigonometric formulas SEE **Math Functions**
Statistics and database formulas SEE **Statistics Functions**
Table lookup and reference function formulas SEE **Lookup Functions**
Text string formulas SEE **Text Functions**
Workbook information formulas SEE **Workbook Functions**

Goal Seek

The Goal Seek command on the Tools menu calculates the **formula** input value that causes the formula to return a specified result. You use Goal Seek when you know what formula result you want but don't know what input value returns that result. To illustrate how the Goal Seek command works, suppose you want to know what regular payment results in a future value formula of $500,000 if the annual interest rate is 10 percent and the term is 25 years.

To use Goal Seek, follow these steps:

1 Build a worksheet that includes the future value formula and that uses cell addresses as inputs. In the example, you want to find the regular payment amount that causes the future value formula in cell B4,=FV(B2,B3,-B1,,1), to return $500,000.

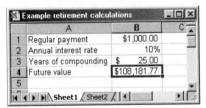

2 Choose the Tools menu's Goal Seek command. Excel displays the Goal Seek dialog box.

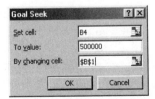

3 Enter the cell address with the formula in the Set Cell text box.

4 Enter the target value you want the formula to return in the To Value text box.

5 Enter the cell address with the input value that the Goal Seek command should adjust in the By Changing Cell text box.

6 Click OK to keep the new values, or click Cancel to restore the old values.

Once you've described the Goal Seek operation, Excel begins adjusting the input value, looking for the value that causes the formula to return the target value. If Goal Seek can find an input value that returns the target value, it displays a message box telling you so and then adjusts the input value cell.

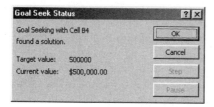

Go To

You can quickly move the **cell selector** to another location by using the Name box or the Edit menu's Go To command.

Using the Name Drop-Down List Box

To quickly move the cell selector to a particular cell, open the Name box. Type the cell address or select a cell name, and then press Enter.

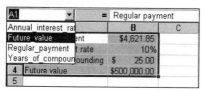

Using the Go To Command

You can also use the Edit menu's Go To command to quickly move to a cell. Excel lists any cell names you've defined in the Go To list box. Double-click any of these to move the cell selector. Or use the Reference text box to enter the address of the cell to which you want to move.

continues

Go To *(continued)*

Using the Go To Dialog Box's Special Button

The Go To dialog box provides a Special button, which you can click to move the cell selector by using cell contents and characteristics. When you click the Special button, Excel displays the Go To Special dialog box. Select the Go To Special dialog box's option buttons to indicate to what kind of cell the selector should be moved. Clicking Formulas, for example, tells Excel to move the selector to the next cell that has a formula.

SEE ALSO **Finding Cells**

Gridlines

Gridlines are the intersecting horizontal and vertical lines that appear on both worksheets and charts.

Gridlines on charts SEE **Chart Gridlines**
Gridlines on printed worksheets SEE **Sheet Page Setup**
Worksheet gridlines appearance and color SEE **Worksheet Views**

Groups

A group is a range selection in two or more **worksheets.** You select a group by making a range selection in the current worksheet and then applying it to additional worksheets by holding down Ctrl and clicking the worksheet **page tabs.** Excel will not display the other worksheets as you click their tabs, but you can tell that a worksheet has been selected because its tabs turn white. Any editing changes you make will apply to all of the selected worksheets.

You can format groups by choosing the Format menu's Cells command. You can fill groups too by choosing the Edit menu's Fill command and then choosing the submenu's Across Worksheets command.

SEE ALSO   Filling Cells; Formatting

Headers and Footers

Choose the File menu's Page Setup command and click the Header/ Footer tab to display a dialog box in which you'll specify how page headers and footers are formatted for printed worksheets and charts.

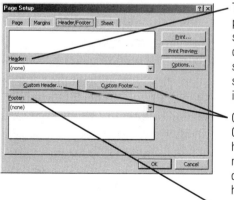

To add a standard header to printed pages, select a header style from the Header drop-down list box. Excel provides standard headers that name the sheet, number pages, and identify the author or user.

Click the Custom Header and Custom Footer buttons to tailor headers or footers to your own needs. Excel displays another dialog box you use to create a header or footer from scratch.

To add a standard footer to printed pages, select a footer style from the Footer drop-down list box.

continues

Headers and Footers *(continued)*

Page headers vs. list headers

Unfortunately, Excel uses the term "header" in two ways. One way refers to the page headers Excel places at the top of printed pages. The other way refers to the column headings that name the fields used in a list.

> **SEE ALSO**   **Sheet Page Setup**

Help

If you need help with Microsoft Excel 2000, you may find it easiest to first try the Office Assistant button on the toolbar. When you click this button, the Office Assistant appears to answer your questions. You can type a question in your own words and, probably, get the answer you need.

If you don't want to use the Office Assistant, right-click the Assistant and choose the shortcut menu's Options command. Clear the Use The Office Assistant check box. Then you can also use the traditional Windows online help system. To take this approach, choose the Help menu's Microsoft Excel Help command. Excel, with Windows' help, displays the Microsoft Excel Help dialog box, where you can peruse the Excel Help file manually.

> **SEE ALSO**   **Office Assistant**

Hiding Formulas SEE Cell Protection

Hiding and Unhiding Sheets

You can hide the active sheet so that it isn't displayed in the workbook window. To do this, choose the Format menu's Sheet command and then choose the submenu's Hide command.

To unhide hidden sheets in the open workbook, choose the Format menu's Sheet command and then choose the submenu's Unhide command. When Excel displays a list of the hidden sheets in the workbook, click the one you want to unhide. Then click OK.

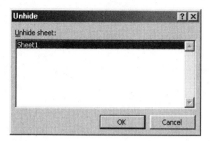

SEE ALSO   Groups

History

Excel maintains a history of the workbooks you've used. You can view this history from either the Open or Save dialog boxes by clicking the History shortcut.

HTML

HTML stands for hypertext markup language. HTML is essentially the language that the Internet uses for web pages. When your web browser displays a web page, for example, what you're really viewing is an HTML document.

It turns out that HTML is also relevant to Microsoft Office 2000. The Office 2000 programs, including Excel, let you save your documents using the traditional binary file format, which previous editions used. But you can also save your documents using the HTML file format. One big benefit of using the HTML file format is that many web browsers (although not all) will be able to view the contents of Office documents that use the HTML file format.

SEE ALSO   Saving Web Pages

Hyperlink

You can insert a link to basically any Internet resource—including World Wide Web pages—or local network resource in your worksheets by choosing the Insert menu's Hyperlink command.

Inserting a Hyperlink

To insert a hyperlink, follow these steps:

1 Select a cell in your worksheet.

2 Enter the text you want to use to identify your hyperlink, and click the Enter button on the formula bar.

3 Choose the Insert menu's Hyperlink command. Or click the Insert Hyperlink toolbar button.

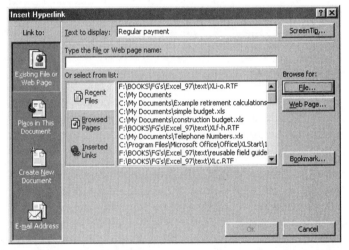

4 If you want the hyperlink to point to a web page or file that you already know the location of, click the Existing File Or Web Page shortcut. Then use the Type The File Or Web Page Name text box to provide the URL or file pathname. Alternatively, if you don't know the URL or file pathname but you have recently opened the web page or file or used it in another hyperlink, click the Recent Files, Browsed Pages, or Inserted Links shortcut, and then select the URL or file pathname from the list box.

Using the Browse For buttons

If you click the Existing File Or Web Page shortcut, you can also click the File button to open a dialog box you can use to locate a file you can't find some other way. And you can click the Web Page button to start Microsoft Internet Explorer, which you can use to locate a web page you can't find some other way.

5 If you want the hyperlink to point to some location in the Excel workbook, click the Place In This Document shortcut. Then enter the cell address in the Type The Cell Reference text box. Alternatively, if you don't know the cell address, select the sheet name or cell name from the Or Select A Place In This Document list box.

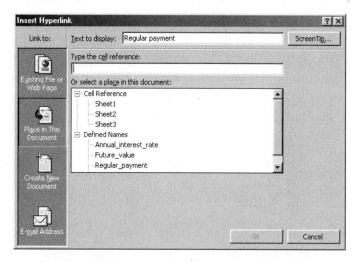

6 If you want the hyperlink to point to a new document that you need to create, click the Create New Document shortcut. Then enter the document's full pathname in the Name Of New Document text box. Select a When To Edit option button to indicate whether you want to begin immediately working with the document or later on.

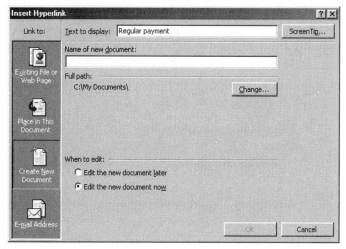

continues

Hyperlink *(continued)*

7 If you want the hyperlink to point to an e-mail address, click the E-Mail Address shortcut. Then enter the person's full e-mail address in the E-Mail Address text box. Enter a brief subject in the Subject text box for the e-mail messages that will be sent when someone clicks this hyperlink. If you don't know the person's e-mail address, you may be able to select the e-mail address from the Recently Used E-Mail Addresses list box.

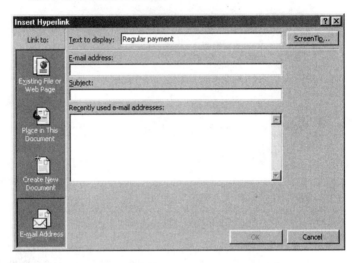

8 Click OK to add the hyperlink.

Using the Hyperlink

After you've inserted a hyperlink, the pointer changes to a hand when it is positioned over the cell containing the hyperlink. Click to open the linked web page. To edit the hyperlink, right-click it and then choose the context menu's Edit Hyperlink command.

Importing Spreadsheet Files

Excel lets you use files created with other spreadsheet programs. To use such a file, choose the File menu's Open command. When Excel displays the Open dialog box, select a file type from the Files Of Type drop-down list box.

SEE ALSO Importing Text Files; Opening Workbooks

Importing Text Files

Excel converts text files—for example, files created with a word processor—for use in an Excel workbook. To convert a text file, follow these steps:

1 Choose the File menu's Open command. Select a file type from the Files Of Type drop-down list box. Then select the text file, and click Open. Excel starts the Text Import Wizard.

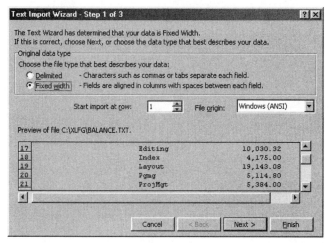

2 Click the Delimited option button if the fields, or blocks, of information are de-limited. ("Delimited" means that the fields are separated with a character such as a tab space.)

3 Click the Fixed Width option button if the fields of information are arranged neatly into fixed-width columns. (A report that tabulates data would almost always be arranged this way, for example.)

4 Tell Excel which is the first line, or row, you want imported.

5 Specify the operating environment in which the file was created: Windows, Macintosh, or MS-DOS. Excel displays the tentative organization of the con-verted text file at the bottom of the dialog box.

6 Click Next.

7 If you are converting a **delimited text file,** use the wizard's second dialog box to identify the delimiter—the character used to separate the blocks of informa-tion on a line. If necessary, select the Treat Consecutive Delimiters As One check box and select an option from the Text Qualifier drop-down list box to adjust for any conversion problems. (A "text qualifier" is the character used by the delimited text file to show the beginning and end of text labels.)

continues

Importing Text Files *(continued)*

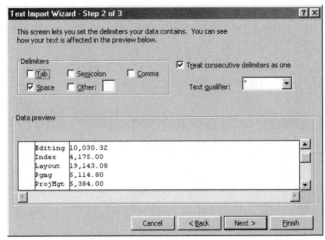

8 If you are converting a nondelimited file, click the mouse to show column borders. Excel adds a vertical arrow to show the border, or break, line. As necessary, remove border lines by double-clicking. As necessary, move border lines by dragging.

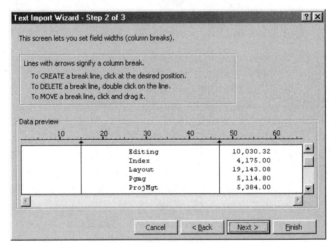

9 Look at the Data Preview area to verify the converted data.

10 Click Next when you've described how to convert the delimited or non-delimited file.

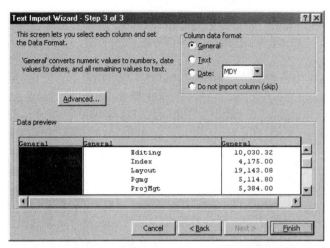

11 Select a column, and then select a Column Data Format option button.

12 Select the Do Not Import Column (Skip) option button if you don't want the text file field in the new Excel workbook.

13 Click Finish to display the converted text file in an Excel workbook. (Once you get the converted text file in an Excel workbook, you'll want to adjust column widths. Also be sure to save the new workbook with the converted text file data.)

For your information

All database and most accounting applications create delimited text files for easy importing into programs such as Microsoft Excel.

> **SEE ALSO   Columns; Saving Workbooks**

Inserting

You can add—or insert—cells, charts, columns, functions, hyperlinks, macros, names, notes, page breaks, pictures, objects, rows, and worksheets.

continues

Inserting *(continued)*

Adding cell comments SEE **Comments**	
Adding cells SEE **Inserting Cells**	
Adding charts SEE **Chart Wizard**	
Adding columns SEE **Inserting Columns**	
Adding functions SEE **Function**	
Adding hyperlinks SEE **Hyperlink**	
Adding macros SEE **Macro**	
Adding names SEE **Names**	
Adding objects SEE **Object**	
Adding page breaks SEE **Page Breaks**	
Adding pictures SEE **Worksheet Pictures**	
Adding rows SEE **Inserting Rows**	
Adding worksheets SEE **Inserting Worksheets**	

Inserting Cells

You can insert single cells or groups of cells into rows and columns.

Inserting a Single Cell

Select the cell that occupies the position you want for the new, inserted cell, choose the Insert menu's Cells command, and then complete the Insert dialog box.

Select an Insert option to indicate how Excel should make room for the new cell or cells: click Shift Cells Down to move the cells in the selected column down, or click Shift Cells Right to move the cells in the selected row to the right.

Don't click the Entire Row or Entire Column option buttons unless you want to insert a row above the active cell or a column to the left of the active cell.

Inserting Several Cells

Select a range of cells so that the top-selected or left-selected cell occupies the position you want for the topmost or leftmost cell in the inserted range. Choose the Insert menu's Cells command, and then complete the Insert dialog box. (Excel inserts as many cells as you select.)

SEE ALSO   Inserting Columns; Inserting Rows

Inserting Columns

You can insert single columns or groups of columns into a worksheet.

Inserting a Single Column

Select the column that occupies the position you want for the inserted column, and then choose the Insert menu's Columns command.

Inserting Several Columns

Select a range of columns so that the leftmost selected column occupies the position you want for the leftmost inserted column, and then choose the Insert menu's Columns command. Excel inserts as many columns as you have selected.

SEE ALSO   Inserting Cells

Inserting Rows

Just as you can insert one or more columns in a worksheet, you can also insert one or more rows.

Inserting a Single Row

Select the row that occupies the position you want for the inserted row, and then choose the Insert menu's Rows command.

Inserting Several Rows

Select a range of rows so that the topmost selected row occupies the position you want for the topmost inserted row, and then choose the Insert menu's Rows command. Excel inserts as many rows as you have selected.

SEE ALSO   Inserting Cells; Inserting Columns

Inserting Worksheets

You can insert as many worksheets as you like in workbooks.

Inserting a Single Worksheet

Select the sheet that occupies the position you want for the inserted worksheet, and then choose the Insert menu's Worksheet command.

Inserting Several Worksheets

Select a range of worksheets by holding down the Shift key and clicking another worksheet tab so that the first selected worksheet occupies the position you want for the first inserted worksheet. Then choose the Insert menu's Worksheet command. Excel inserts as many worksheets as you have selected.

SEE ALSO   Inserting Cells

Installing Excel

Microsoft Office 2000 is very smart about the way it installs Excel and the other Office programs on your computer. For example, the Office setup program looks at your computer and any previous installations before it installs Excel, in order to install only those parts of Excel that you're likely to use. And if some piece of the Excel program becomes damaged or necessary, Excel will automatically repair itself by reinstalling damaged components or installing missing components. For these reasons, you may occasionally find yourself prompted to supply the Office CD or Excel CD.

SEE ALSO   Detect And Repair

Italic Characters

You can *italicize* characters in the current worksheet selection by pressing Ctrl+I or by clicking the Italic toolbar button. You can also choose the Format menu's Cells command and select options on the Font tab.

SEE ALSO   Changing Fonts

Labels

A label is something you enter in a cell but that you don't want to use later in a formula. Usually a label is a block of text or a block of text and numbers. But a label might use numbers and still not be something you later want to use in a formula. For example, a telephone number uses numbers, but you probably wouldn't ever use a telephone number in a formula.

SEE ALSO   Entering Data; Values

Laptop Computers

If you're using Excel on a laptop computer, you should know that almost everything described here, in this book, applies with equal force to your computing environment. You should also consider two other, minor points. First, because pointing devices on a laptop are often challenging to use, remember that everything you want to do can also be accomplished with your keyboard. You can activate the menu bar, for example, by pressing Alt. And once you've done this, you can select menus and commands by pressing the underlined letter or number in their names.

A second point to remember if you're using a laptop is that some of Excel's installation features won't work on your laptop unless you have access to the original Excel installation information—such as the original installation CD. As described in the **Installing Excel** and **Detect And Repair** entries, Excel may need to install additional components of the program as you work or may need to repair damaged components of the program.

List Management

Excel provides a simple database management feature called List Management. You can use it to sort lists, filter them, and subtotal list entries. And you can use it to create PivotTables based on lists.

continues

List Management *(continued)*

Analyzing lists SEE **PivotTable and PivotChart**

Arranging and organizing lists SEE **Sorting Lists**

Building lists SEE **Creating Lists**

Creating a new list using a list SEE **Filtering Lists**

Editing entries in a list SEE **Editing Lists**

Finding a list entry SEE **Searching Lists**

Removing, or deleting, entries from a list SEE **Editing Lists**

Lookup Functions

Lookup functions return specified values or labels from tables or arrays. For example, the following function returns the second label—which is CA—in the array of labels included as arguments.

Lookup formulas specify which value or label should be returned using one argument.

=CHOOSE(2,"AZ","CA","ID","MT")

Lookup formulas also specify where the function should look for the specified value or label.

SEE ALSO   Argument; Function

Lotus 1-2-3

Lotus 1-2-3 is another spreadsheet program—as you may know. What you may not know is that you can open and save Lotus 1-2-3 worksheet files with Excel. To do this, specify a Lotus 1-2-3 file format in the Open and Save dialog boxes' List Files Of Type list boxes.

SEE ALSO   Importing Spreadsheet Files; Opening Workbooks; Saving Workbooks

Macro

A macro is made up of a series of commands, which means that a macro is really a simple program. Macros are very handy because they let you automate tasks within Excel. For example, if you find yourself repeating some action numerous times, you can save yourself some keystrokes by writing a macro that automates the action.

Recording a Macro

The easiest way to write a macro is to tell Excel it should record the sequence of steps you want to automate. To do this, follow these steps:

1 Choose the Tools menu's Macro command, and then choose the submenu's Record New Macro command. Excel displays the Record Macro dialog box.

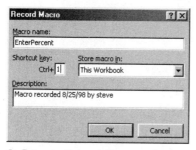

2 Enter a self-descriptive name for the macro in the Macro Name text box.

3 Optionally, provide a letter in the Shortcut Key text box that you can use, in combination with the Ctrl key, to tell Excel it should run the macro.

4 Indicate in which Excel workbook the macro should be stored in the Store Macro In text box. Typically, you'll store the macro in the workbook in which you usually run the macro.

5 Click OK. Excel closes the Record Macro dialog box and displays the Macro toolbar, which provides two buttons: Stop and Relative Reference. Click the Stop button to tell Excel when it should stop recording your actions. Click the Relative Reference button to tell Excel that it should consider your cell selections to be relative references rather than absolute references.

6 Perform the exact sequence of actions you want Excel to record.

7 Click the Macro toolbar's Stop button.

Writing a Macro from Scratch

You can write macros from scratch using Microsoft's **Visual Basic** for Applications programming language. Note, however, that Visual Basic programming, while not overly difficult, is more involved than most Excel users will have time for. To comfortably program in Visual Basic, you really need to learn both about structured programming and the Visual Basic development environment.

continues

Macro *(continued)*

Running a Macro

You can run a macro in two ways: If you created a shortcut key combination for the macro, run the macro by pressing Ctrl and the letter key you specified as the shortcut. You can also run a macro by choosing the Tools menu's Macro command and then choosing the submenu's Macros command. When Excel displays the Macro dialog box, double-click the macro you want to run.

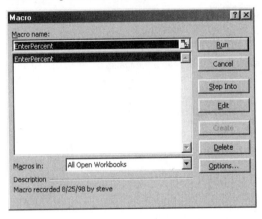

Margins

Choose the File menu's Page Setup command and click the Margins tab to display a dialog box in which you can specify page margins for printed worksheets and charts.

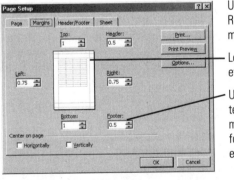

Use the Top, Bottom, Left and Right boxes to specify the margins in inches.

Look at the preview to see the effect of your specifications.

Use the Header and Footer text boxes to specify how many inches a header and footer should be from the edge of the page.

SEE ALSO   Headers and Footers; Printing

Math Functions

Excel's rich set of arithmetic, logarithmic, and trigonometric functions make for quick mathematical **formulas**. Here's a sampling of what they can do:

Function	What it does
=COS(.5)	Returns the cosine of 0.5, which is 0.877582562.
=LOG10(100)	Returns the common logarithm of 100, which is 2.
=SQRT(9)	Returns the square root of 9, which is 3.

SEE ALSO   Argument; AutoSum; Function

Microsoft Query

Microsoft Query is the name of another program that comes with Excel. Query lets you query, or extract information, from external databases, such as those created in Microsoft Access. To use Query, choose the Data menu's Get External Data command and then choose a submenu command. To describe a query, for example, choose the New Data Query command.

SEE ALSO   Web Query

Microsoft Word SEE Word

Moving and Copying Sheets

You can shuffle the sheets in a workbook by moving (and copying) them. To move or copy a sheet, follow the steps on the next page.

continues

Moving and Copying Sheets *(continued)*

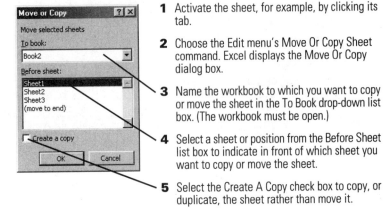

1 Activate the sheet, for example, by clicking its tab.

2 Choose the Edit menu's Move Or Copy Sheet command. Excel displays the Move Or Copy dialog box.

3 Name the workbook to which you want to copy or move the sheet in the To Book drop-down list box. (The workbook must be open.)

4 Select a sheet or position from the Before Sheet list box to indicate in front of which sheet you want to copy or move the sheet.

5 Select the Create A Copy check box to copy, or duplicate, the sheet rather than move it.

SEE ALSO   **Chart Sheets; Worksheets**

Moving Data

You can move data—values, labels, formulas, and worksheet ranges—with either the mouse or the Edit menu's Cut and Paste commands.

Moving Data with the Mouse

To move data with the mouse, select what you want to move, click the selection border, and then drag the selection.

Moving Data with Cut and Paste

To move data with the Cut and Paste commands, follow these steps:

1 Select the cell or worksheet range you want to move.

2 Choose the Edit menu's Cut command, or click the Cut toolbar button.

3 Select the cell to which the copied cell should be moved, or select the cell to which the upper left corner cell of the worksheet range should be moved.

4 Choose the Edit menu's Paste command, or click the Paste toolbar button.

Moving formulas

When you move a formula, Excel doesn't adjust relative **cell references** in it.

SEE ALSO   **Copying Data; Copying Formulas**

Moving Objects and Pictures

You can move objects and pictures with the mouse or with commands.

Moving with the Mouse

Simply select the object or picture, and then drag it where you want it.

Excel adds selection handles to the object or picture to show you've selected it. The selection handles are the little squares that appear at the corners and along each edge.

Moving with Commands

You can also move a graphic object or picture by using the Edit menu's Cut and Paste commands in the same way you move other types of worksheet data.

SEE ALSO   Copying Objects and Pictures; Pictures; Resizing; Pictures

My Documents

Windows supplies a folder, named My Documents, that it expects you'll use for storing many of the documents you create. Based on this assumption, Excel's Open and Save dialog boxes both provide a My Documents shortcut that you can use to quickly open the My Documents folder.

Names

You can name a cell or a range of cells and then refer to that name in **formulas** and in command dialog boxes. To name a cell, follow these steps:

	A	B	C	D
Plywood		=	76.42	
1		Actual	Budget	
2	2 x 4s	35.67	40	
3	Plywood	76.42	80	
4	Nails	1.95	2	
5	Total	114.04		
6				

1 Select the cell or range of cells.

2 Click the formula bar's Name box.

3 Enter the cell or range name in the Name box.

SEE ALSO   Formula Bar

Naming Sheets

Excel provides default names for **worksheets** and **chart sheets**—Sheet1, Sheet2, Chart1, and so on—but these names aren't very descriptive. Fortunately, you can use sheet names to organize your workbooks. To replace Excel's default names, double-click the sheet tab, or choose the Format menu's Sheet command and then choose the submenu's Rename command.

25		
26		
27		

Budget / Sheet2 / Sheet3 /

Replace the existing sheet name by typing over it.

Natural Language Formulas

You can write **formulas** using cell **labels**. Here's an example.

B4	▼	=	=Gross-Cost

	A	B	C	D	E
1		Year 1	Year 2	Year 3	
2	Gross	100000	80000	110000	
3	Cost	30000	25000	32000	
4	Net	70000	55000	78000	
5					

Enter the formula =Gross-Cost in cell B4. Excel correctly interprets your formula as if you had entered =B2-B3.

New Workbooks

To create a new workbook, choose the File menu's New command or click the New toolbar button. If you click the New toolbar button, Excel just opens a new, blank worksheet. If you choose the File menu's New command, Excel displays the New dialog box, which you can use to indicate that you want Excel to create your new workbook based on an existing workbook template. (Excel comes with several of these.) To select a template, find the New dialog box tab that the template's icon appears on and then double-click the icon.

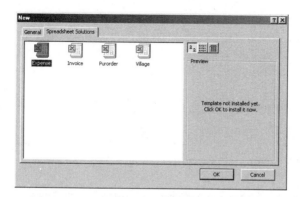

SEE ALSO   Opening Workbooks; Saving Workbooks; Workbooks

Object

You can use objects to create what's called a "compound document"—a document file that combines two or more types of information. For example, you might want to create a compound document that includes a long report written in, for example, Microsoft Word or WordPerfect. On page 27 of your report, however, you might want to include a worksheet or worksheet fragment created in Excel. On page 37 of your report, you might want to include a chart created in Excel. So your compound document consists of portions of information created in different programs— portions called objects—and pasted together into one big compound document.

Creating Compound Documents

To do all this pasting and combining, you can often use the program's Copy and Paste (or Paste Special) commands on the Edit menu. And if you're creating the compound document in Excel, you can use the Insert menu's Object command.

Distinguishing Between Linked Objects and Embedded Objects

A linked object—remember that it might be the Excel worksheet you've pasted into a word-processing document—gets updated whenever the source document changes. An embedded object doesn't. (You can, however, double-click an embedded object to open the application that created the embedded object to make your changes.)

continues

Object *(continued)*

Let me also make what may be an obvious point. If you embed, or copy, an object into a compound document, it gets bigger. When you simply link an object, the compound document doesn't really get bigger.

What you absolutely need to know about objects

Perhaps the most important tidbit for you to know about objects is that they're very easy to use. You don't have to do anything other than copy and paste the objects you want to insert in the compound document.

SEE ALSO   **Embedding and Linking Existing Objects; Embedding New Objects**

Office Assistant

Microsoft Excel's help can be supplied by the Office Assistant, an animated character that pops up whenever you click the Office Assistant button, or by choosing the Help menu's Detect And Repair command. When the Assistant appears, type a question and click Search. The Assistant will display the help topics that most closely relate to your question. Or click Tips, and the Assistant will display a series of tips that help you get the most out of Excel.

	A	B	C	D	E	F	G	H
1		Year 1	Year 2	Year 3				
2	Gross	100000	80000	110000				
3	Cost	30000	25000	32000				
4	Net	70000	55000	78000				
5								
6								
7					**What would you like to do?**			
8								
9					How do I calculate a loan			
10					payment?			
11					Options Search			
12								
13								
14								
15								
16								
17								
18								
19								

Customizing the Assistant

You can customize the Office Assistant to suit your preferences using the Office Assistant dialog box. To pick the particular Assistant you like, right-click the Assistant and choose the shortcut menu's Choose Assistant command. You can choose an Assistant from a gallery of available characters on the Gallery tab of the Office Assistant dialog box. Your choices range from a robot to an Albert Einstein look-alike.

Setting Assistant Options

By choosing the shortcut menu's Options command, you display the Options tab of the Office Assistant dialog box, where you can set a variety of options relating to the Assistant's capabilities. You can also set options that control how tips are displayed.

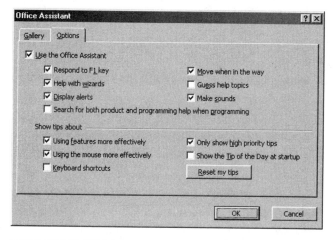

Hiding the Assistant

Microsoft research indicates that people either strongly like or dislike the Office Assistant. If you find yourself in the latter category, right-click the Office Assistant and choose the shortcut menu's Hide command to remove the Assistant from your window until the next time you choose Help. To prevent the Assistant from reappearing, right-click the Assistant and choose the shortcut menu's Options command. Clear the Use The Office Assistant check box.

SEE ALSO   Help

O

Office Server Extensions

The newest version of Excel works with Office Server Extensions. Office Server Extensions and a related feature called WebPost, which is available in each of the Microsoft Office 2000 programs, let you save and retrieve Office documents from a web server as well as collaborate on documents. Note, however, that Office Server Extensions should be transparent to Excel users. The Office Server Extensions aren't something Excel users need to work with directly. Office Server Extensions run on the web server and typically are monitored and maintained by the network or web server administrator.

SEE ALSO   HTML; Opening Workbooks; Saving Web Pages; Saving Workbooks

Opening Workbooks

To open a previously saved workbook, choose the File menu's Open command or click the Open toolbar button. Either way, Excel displays the Open dialog box, as shown below.

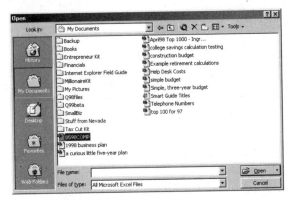

1 Click the **History, My Documents, Desktop, Favorites,** or **Web Folders** shortcut icon to specify where the workbook is located if you've previously saved, opened, or viewed the file; stored it in the My Documents folder; stored it on your desktop; added it to your Favorites folder; or retrieved it from a web folder. Or, alternatively, specify where the workbook file was saved in the Look In text box.

2 If necessary, select a file type from the Files Of Type list box if you want to open a file with a format other than that of the usual Excel workbook file. (You might do this if you want to import another spreadsheet program's file.)

3 When you see the workbook file in the file list box, double-click it to open it. Or, alternatively, enter the workbook's name in the File Name text box, and click Open.

Protecting the original workbook

If you don't want to overwrite the original workbook file, click the down arrow at the right end of the Open button and then choose the drop-down menu's Open Read Only command. (If you choose Open Read Only and later want to save the workbook, you'll need to use a new filename.) If you want to open a copy of the original workbook file, click the down arrow at the right end of the Open button and then choose the drop-down menu's Open As Copy command. If you just want to browse a workbook you've saved using the HTML file format, click the down arrow at the right end of the Open button and then choose the drop-down menu's Open In Browser command.

> **SEE ALSO**   Default Workbooks; File Properties; Saving Workbooks; Troubleshooting: You Can't Find a File

---

Orienting Labels and Values SEE Aligning Labels and Values

Outlining

Excel has an outlining feature that lets you work with a worksheet as an outline—just as most word processors let you work with documents as outlines. In essence, what Outlining lets you do is hide detail. If you briefly review the workbook that follows, for example, you'll notice that individual operating expense categories roll up into departments, that departments roll up into divisions, and that divisions roll up into the company. With Outlining, an Excel user can create an easy way of hiding operating-expense-detail or of hiding operating-expense-level detail and department-level detail—or of hiding even division-level detail.

continues

Outlining *(continued)*

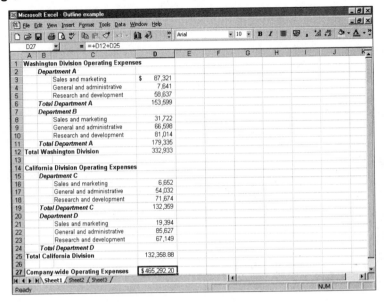

Creating an Outline

To create an outline, follow these steps:

1 Select the first set of rows that you will most often want to hide—in other words, select the lowest level of the outline. In the example workbook shown above you would select rows 2, 3, 4, and 5.

2 Choose the Data menu's Group And Outline command, and then choose the submenu's Group command.

3 Repeat steps 1 and 2 for each of the other sets of rows that you want most often want to hide because they also represent the lowest level of the outline. In the example workbook shown above, you would also select rows 7, 8, 9, and 10, and then choose the Group command; select rows 15, 16, 17, and 18, and then choose the Group command; and select rows 20, 21, 22, and 23, and then choose the Group command.

4 Repeat steps 1, 2, and 3 for each of the other, higher level sets of rows that you most often want to hide. For example, in the workbook shown above, you could create division-level groupings using rows 1 to 11 and rows 14 to 24. And you could create a company-level grouping using rows 1 to 26.

Working with an Outline

When you finish grouping rows, you work with an outline largely by clicking the outline buttons, which appear along the left edge of the workbook window. To collapse a group, for example, click the Minus button. To later expand that group, click the Plus button, which appears after you click the Minus button. Note that you can remove an outline by choosing the Data menu's Group And Outline command and then choosing the submenu's Clear Outline command.

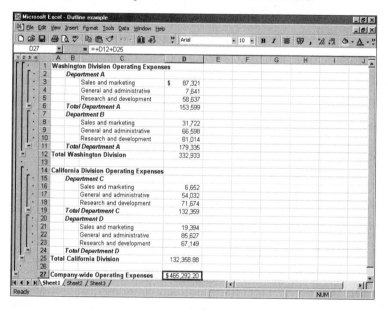

Page Break Preview

Page Break Preview lets you see where the page breaks will fall in a worksheet you intend to print. In Page Break Preview mode, you can click and drag page breaks where you want them in your worksheet. To open the Page Break Preview mode, choose the View menu's Page Break Preview command. Choose the View menu's Normal command to return to the Normal worksheet view.

SEE ALSO   Page Breaks

Page Breaks

Excel breaks worksheets into page-size portions automatically as it prints, drawing a dashed line wherever page breaks occur. You can let Excel determine these page breaks, or you can choose where these page breaks occur.

Adding Vertical Page Breaks

Select the column just to the right of where the worksheet should be vertically split into separate pages, and then choose the Insert menu's Page Break command.

Adding Horizontal Page Breaks

Select the row just below where the worksheet should be horizontally split into separate pages, and then choose the Insert menu's Page Break command.

Removing Page Breaks

Select the column just to the right of or the row just below the page break, and then choose the Insert menu's Remove Page Break command.

SEE ALSO Printing

Page Numbers

You add page numbers to printed worksheets and charts by adding a header or a footer that includes a page number. You can even specify which number Excel uses for the first page. For example, the first page of a printed worksheet shouldn't be numbered 1 if it's the 26th page in a report; it should be numbered 26.

SEE ALSO Headers and Footers; Printed Pages Setup

Page Setup

Choose the File menu's Page Setup command, and click its tabs—Page, Margins, Header/Footer, Sheet, and Chart—to display pages with options to control the appearance of printed worksheets and charts.

Chart appearance SEE **Chart Page Setup**
Page appearance SEE **Printed Pages Setup**
Page headers and page footers SEE **Headers and Footers**
Page margins SEE **Margins**
Sheet appearance SEE **Sheet Page Setup**

Page Tab

Excel uses page tabs in several ways. One use is to label the workbook sheet. (You can also click sheet page tabs to move through a workbook.) Another use of page tabs appears in some dialog boxes. If a dialog box shows more than will fit within its border, the dialog box includes tabs for going to other pages. On each page is a set of needed input information.

You move through these pages by clicking the page tabs. To see an example of how this works, choose the File menu's Page Setup command and then click the page tabs—Page, Margins, Header/Footer, Sheet, and Chart.

SEE ALSO   Naming Sheets

Pagination

Pagination refers to the process of breaking a document into page-size portions. You can let Excel paginate your documents. You do this simply by printing the workbook or by print-previewing the workbook. Or you can do it yourself using hard page breaks. You do this by choosing the Insert menu's Page Break command.

SEE ALSO   Page Breaks; Printing; Print Preview

Passwords

You can use passwords to limit access to workbooks, to limit changes to workbook files, and to limit changes to cell contents.

Controlling access to workbook files SEE **Save Options**

Protecting cells in a workbook SEE **Cell Protection**

Paste Function SEE **Function**

Pathname

A pathname describes the location of a file on your computer or, if you're working on a local area network, on the network. Office programs such as Excel let you use pathnames when **opening workbooks** and **saving workbooks**—you simply enter the pathname in the File Name box. You can also sometimes enter a pathname in place of a URL—for example, when you use the **web query** feature.

A pathname typically consists of three parts: the disk drive letter, the folder name, and the filename. If a file named letters.htm is stored in a folder named correspondence and this folder is located on the C disk drive, the pathname is

c:\correspondence\letters.htm

Note that the disk drive letter is separated from the folder name by a colon and backslash and that the folder name is separated from the filename by a backslash.

If a file is located in a subfolder, the subfolder or subfolders become part of the pathname, too. For example, if a file named letters.htm is stored in a subfolder named January, which is stored in a folder named correspondence which is located on the C disk drive, the pathname is

c:\correspondence\january\letters.htm

Patterns

To add background patterns to cells, choose the Format menu's Cells command and then click the Patterns tab. When Excel displays its palette of patterns, select the foreground color for the pattern using the colored Cell Shading buttons. Then, select a pattern and a color for the lines, dots, or cross-hatching that create the pattern from the Pattern drop-down list box.

SEE ALSO   Coloring Worksheet Ranges

Percentages

Percentages are decimal values such as 0.75 formatted as 75%. To store percentages in cells, enter them as decimal values and then format them, or enter them as percentages. (In this case, Excel stores the decimal value in the cell but formats the decimal value as a percentage.)

SEE ALSO   Entering Data; Formatting Numbers; Fractions

Personal Menus and Toolbars

Excel 2000 combines tools from the Standard toolbar and the Formatting toolbar to create a new Personal toolbar that is displayed beneath the menu bar. Excel further customizes toolbars and menus by hiding toolbar buttons and commands you don't use and displaying those you do use. Usually, this **adaptability** feature enhances your use of Excel because toolbars and menus are less cluttered. If you don't find personalized menus and toolbars helpful, you can override the way Excel modifies them by following the instructions located in the Troubleshooting section of this Pocket Guide.

SEE ALSO   Troubleshooting: Your Menu Commands Disappear *and* Your Toolbar Buttons Appear or Disappear

Picture Charts

A picture chart uses little pictures in place of standard chart **data markers** such as pie slices, bars, and lines. You can replace the standard data markers Excel uses for charts with clip-art images. To create a picture chart, follow these steps:

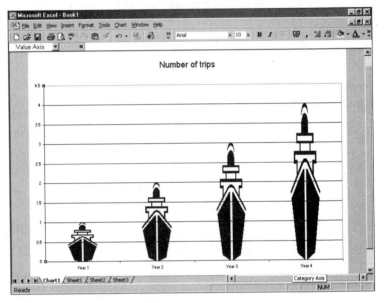

1 Plot your data in a bar, column, or line chart.

2 Copy to the Clipboard the picture you want to use in place of the standard data marker. (You can do this by inserting a picture in an Excel workbook, selecting the picture, and then choosing the Edit menu's Copy command.)

3 Display the chart.

4 Select the data markers you want to replace by clicking them.

5 Choose the Edit menu's Paste command.

SEE ALSO   Clipboard; Pictures

Pictures

Excel comes with a rich clip-art library of images you can add to your workbooks. To add a clip-art image to a workbook, choose the Insert menu's Pictures command and then choose the submenu's ClipArt command. When Excel displays the Insert ClipArt dialog box, click the Pictures tab and then scroll to find first the image category and then the actual image you want to insert. After you've found the image, click it, and then click the Insert Clip toolbar button.

SEE ALSO **Copying Objects and Pictures; Moving Objects and Pictures; Resizing Pictures**

PivotChart SEE PivotTable and PivotChart

PivotTable and PivotChart

Both Excel's PivotTable and PivotChart let you easily organize, reorganize, and analyze worksheet data simply by running a wizard and then dragging buttons. While using a PivotTable or PivotChart is simple, however, these two tools can give you powerful new insights into worksheet data that can be viewed from a variety of perspectives.

Setting Up a PivotTable or PivotChart Worksheet

You create PivotTables for lists such as the worksheet shown below.

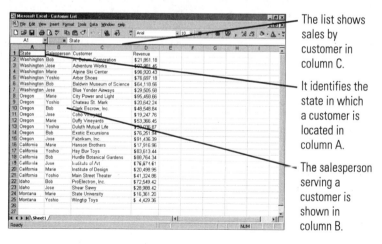

The list shows sales by customer in column C.

It identifies the state in which a customer is located in column A.

The salesperson serving a customer is shown in column B.

Running the PivotTable or PivotChart Wizard

Once you have your worksheet set up, you create PivotTables and PivotCharts by using a wizard. To run the wizard, follow the steps on the following page.

continues

PivotTable and PivotChart *(continued)*

1 Select the list (including the column headings, or headers). In the worksheet shown earlier, for example, you would select the range A1:D25.

2 Choose the Data menu's PivotTable And PivotChart Report command. Excel starts the PivotTable And PivotChart Wizard.

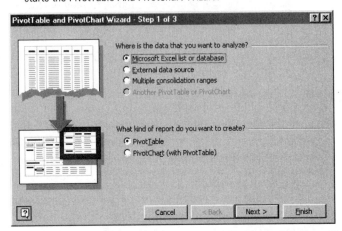

3 Indicate the source you'll use for creating the PivotTable. Usually you'll use a list, so click the first option button. You can also use an external data source, another PivotTable, or a consolidated range. Indicate whether you want to create a PivotTable or a PivotChart by clicking one of the What Kind Of Report Do You Want To Create? option buttons. Click Next.

4 Confirm the data source, and then click Next. If you use a list, for example, the second PivotTable Wizard dialog box asks for the worksheet range containing the list. (The appearance of the second PivotTable Wizard dialog box depends on the data source used for the PivotTable.) Optionally, click Browse to display a dialog box you can use to open another workbook file—if that's where the list is located. Click Next.

5 Indicate where you want the PivotTable or PivotChart stored. If you want the new report stored on a new sheet, Excel adds the sheet. If you want it stored on an existing sheet, give the name of the sheet and the cell reference from the top left corner of the worksheet selection, such as Sheet2!A1. Click Finish. Excel creates either an empty PivotTable or PivotChart report.

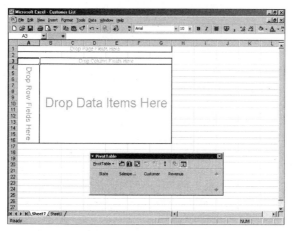

6 If you indicated you want to create a PivotTable, Excel displays a blank PivotTable worksheet. Drag the button for the list field you want to summarize to the Drop Data Items Here block. By default, the PivotTable And PivotChart Wizard assumes you want to sum values and count labels. But double-click any list field button to display a dialog box you can use to select another summary calculation. Drag the button for the list field that should show in rows to the Drop Row Fields Here block. To arrange list information on separate worksheet pages or in separate columns, drag buttons to the Drop Page Fields Here or Drop Column Fields Here blocks. After you finish arranging list information into rows, pages, and columns, Excel creates the PivotTable.

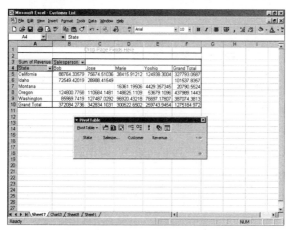

7 If you indicated you want to create a PivotChart, Excel displays a blank PivotChart sheet. Drag the button for the list field you want to summarize to the Drop Data Items Here block. By default, the PivotTable And PivotChart Wizard assumes you want to sum values and count labels.

continues

PivotTable and PivotChart *(continued)*

8 Double-click any list field button to display a dialog box you can use to select another summary calculation.

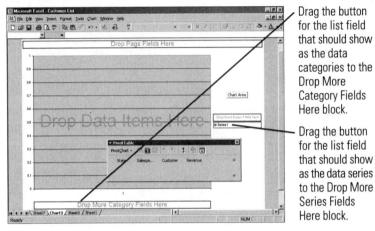

Drag the button for the list field that should show as the data categories to the Drop More Category Fields Here block.

Drag the button for the list field that should show as the data series to the Drop More Series Fields Here block.

9 To arrange list information on separate sheet pages, drag a button to the Drop Page Fields Here block. After you finish arranging list information into rows, columns, and pages, Excel creates the PivotChart.

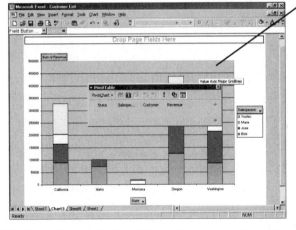

A completed PivotChart looks like this.

10 Optionally, click the PivotTable toolbar button and then choose the Table Options command to display the PivotTable Options dialog box. Select the Format Options and Data Source Options check boxes to indicate where grand totals should be calculated, whether the PivotTable data should be saved, and whether Excel should AutoFormat the table.

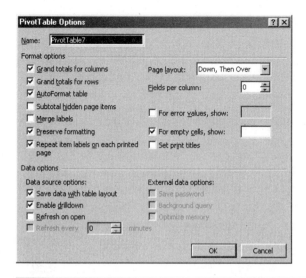

Changing PivotTable and PivotChart Organization

You can change the organization of a PivotTable or PivotChart by dragging the list field buttons to new locations. Your best bet for gaining a better appreciation of how all this works is simply to experiment. Note that you may want to save your workbook before you begin making changes because the saved workbook will provide an easy way to return to your original PivotTable or PivotChart report.

Working with the PivotTable Toolbar

The PivotTable toolbar provides a menu and several commands useful for working with PivotTable reports and PivotChart reports. When you point to a button, Excel displays a ScreenTip that describes what the button does.

SEE ALSO   Creating Lists

Points

One point equals 1/72 inch. In Excel, you specify font size and row height in points. Note, however, that a 12-point font won't fit in a row measuring 12 points in height. For this reason, your row height point-size setting needs to exceed your font point-size setting.

SEE ALSO   Fonts; Rows

Precedents

Precedents are cells that supply other cells' formulas with values. For example, if the formula in cell A1 references cells B12 and E6, the values in cells B12 and E6 must be supplied before the formula in A1 calculates. Cells B12 and E6, then, are precedent cells for A1.

SEE ALSO **Auditing Worksheets; Dependents**

Printed Pages Setup

Choose the File menu's Page Setup command and click the Page tab to display the dialog box you use to specify how pages should print.

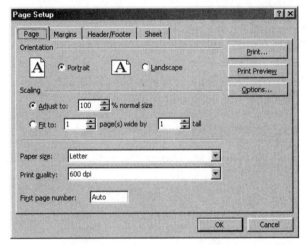

1 Select an Orientation option to specify whether pages should be printed portrait or landscape.

2 Select a Scaling option, and enter an amount in the text box or boxes to change the size of the printed worksheet or chart by a set percentage.

3 Select a paper size from the Paper Size drop-down list box (assuming your printer supports this), and select a setting from the Print Quality drop-down list box to change the print quality.

4 Tell Excel the page number to assign to the first printed page by using the First Page Number text box.

Printing

To print the worksheet or chart displayed in a workbook window, choose the File menu's Print command or click the Print toolbar button.

If you choose the Print command, Excel displays the Print dialog box. Use it to control how Excel prints the worksheet or chart.

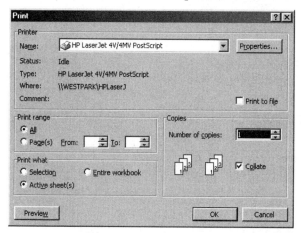

1 Select a Print What option to indicate whether you want to print the Selection (just the currently selected worksheet range), the Active Sheet(s) (the sheet that shows plus any others you've selected by pressing Ctrl or Shift and clicking), or the Entire Workbook (all the worksheets and charts in the workbook).

2 Select a Print Range option, and if necessary, enter page numbers in the text boxes to indicate whether Excel should print all the pages you've indicated by your Print What setting (the usual case) or only a range of pages indicated by your Print What setting.

3 Click OK to print the worksheet.

SEE ALSO   **Printed Pages Setup; Print Preview**

Print Preview

You can choose the File menu's Print Preview command or click the Print Preview toolbar button to see how a workbook's pages will look before you print them. When you choose the command, Excel displays the Print Preview window.

continues

Print Preview (continued)

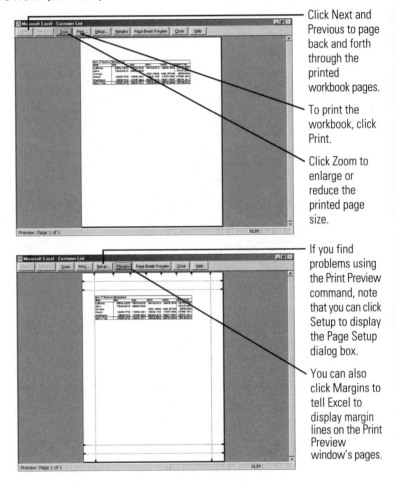

Click Next and Previous to page back and forth through the printed workbook pages.

To print the workbook, click Print.

Click Zoom to enlarge or reduce the printed page size.

If you find problems using the Print Preview command, note that you can click Setup to display the Page Setup dialog box.

You can also click Margins to tell Excel to display margin lines on the Print Preview window's pages.

SEE ALSO   Printed Pages Setup; Printing

Range Address

A range address identifies the cells included in a rectangular portion of a worksheet. A range address consists of the upper left and lower right corner cell addresses, separated by a colon.

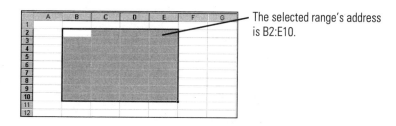

The selected range's address is B2:E10.

Lotus 1-2-3 and range addresses

If you've looked up this entry because you're a Lotus 1-2-3 user and you're having trouble specifying range addresses in Excel, let me make an observation. Your problem—if you want to call it that—probably isn't that you can't figure out how to type some range address such as B2:E10. Your problem is that, in Excel, you need to select the range before you choose commands rather than after you choose them. For example, to erase the contents of the range B2:E10 in Excel, select the range and then choose the Edit menu's Clear command. In comparison, in Lotus 1-2-3, choose the Range Erase command first, and then specify the range B2..E10.

Redo

You can usually repeat your last change to a workbook by choosing the Edit menu's Repeat command or by clicking the Redo toolbar button.

SEE ALSO Undo

Relative Cell Address

A relative cell address is a **cell address** that Excel adjusts if it's part of a copied formula. While relative cell addresses may sound complicated, they really aren't, as an example shows. In the worksheet fragment that follows, cell A2 holds the formula =A1*1.05.

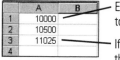

Excel assumes the cell address in the formula, A1, is relative to the formula location in cell A2.

If you copy the formula from cell A2 to cell A3, Excel adjusts the formula to read =A2*1.05. Because you've moved the formula down one row, Excel moves all the formula cell addresses down one row, too.

SEE ALSO Absolute Cell Address; Copying Formulas; Formulas

Removing Styles

To remove, or delete, a **style,** follow these steps:

1 Choose the Format menu's Style command. Excel displays the Style dialog box.

2 Select the style from the Style Name box.

3 Click Delete.

SEE ALSO   Adding Styles

Replacing Cell Contents

Choose the Edit menu's Replace command to locate cells with specified contents—a fragment of text, part of a formula, a cell name, a cell address, or a value—and then replace these contents. To use the Replace command, follow these steps:

1 Select the worksheet range Excel should search.

2 Choose the Edit menu's Replace command. Excel displays the Replace dialog box.

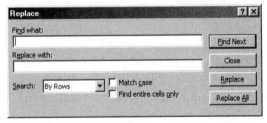

3 Enter what you want to replace in the Find What text box.

4 Enter the replacement content in the Replace With text box.

5 Indicate whether Excel should search column by column or row by row in the Search drop-down list box.

6 Select the Match Case and Find Entire Cells Only check boxes to indicate whether Excel should consider case (lower vs. upper) in its search and look for entire cells rather than parts of cells.

7 Click Find Next to start and restart the search.

8 Click Replace to insert the replacement text in the active cell.

9 Click Replace All to insert the replacement text in all cells in the selected area.

SEE ALSO   Finding Cells

Reports

A report describes the worksheet or worksheet ranges you want to print. If you've created views and scenarios, you can also include different views or scenarios in a report. To create and use reports, use the Report Manager. (To install the Report Manager add-in, choose the Tools menu's Add-Ins command, select the Report Manager check box, and click OK.) After you install the add-in, Excel adds the Report Manager command to the View menu. You use it to create and print reports.

Resizing Pictures

Use the mouse to resize drawing objects and pictures. To do this, select the object or picture. Excel marks the object or picture with selection handles. The selection handles, as you may already know, are those little black or white squares. To change the object's or picture's size, drag the selection handles.

SEE ALSO   Copying Objects and Pictures; Moving Objects and Pictures; Pictures

Rows

You can change the height of rows by using the mouse or by choosing the Format menu's Row command and then choosing submenu commands. Using the mouse is usually easier. To change the height of a selected row or of several selected rows with the mouse, drag the bottom edge of the row label up or down.

Drag the bottom edge of the row label either up or down to change a row's height. Excel changes the mouse pointer to a two-directional arrow when you position the mouse pointer on the bottom edge.

SEE ALSO   Columns

Save Options

The Save As dialog box provides a Tools button, which displays a menu of commands. You can use two of the commands, Web Options and General Options, to manage the way Excel saves workbooks.

Specifying Web Options

To control how HTML versions of an Excel document should be saved, click the Tools toolbar button and then choose the Web Options command. When Excel displays the Web Options dialog box, use its General tab to specify the appearance and compatibility of the document, its File tab to specify filename and location settings, its Pictures tab to specify graphics file format and target monitor information, and the Encoding tab to specify which alphabet should be used.

Specifying General Options

To set up a password and other file security measures, click the Tools toolbar button and then choose the General Options command. When Excel displays the General Options dialog box, follow these steps:

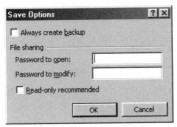

1 Select the Always Create Backup check box to create a backup copy of the existing, or old, workbook file whenever you save a new copy of the workbook file.

2 Limit viewing of the file by assigning a password in the Password To Open text box. Excel asks for the password when someone attempts to open the workbook file by choosing the File menu's Open command.

3 Limit changes to the file by assigning a password in the Password To Modify text box. Excel asks for the password when someone attempts to open the workbook file. Anyone who doesn't know the password can open the file only as Read Only. (However, someone can still save a copy of the workbook file with a new name.)

4 Select the Read-Only Recommended check box if you want Excel to display a message that suggests someone open the file with read-only privileges. By opening the workbook file as read-only, you can't save it later except by giving it a new name.

SEE ALSO **File Properties; Saving Workbooks**

Saving Web Pages

You can save workbooks or workbook selections as web pages, even to the point of publishing a workbook or workbook selection to a web server so that other people can use the workbook. To save a workbook or workbook selection as a web page, choose the File menu's Save As Web Page command and then follow these steps:

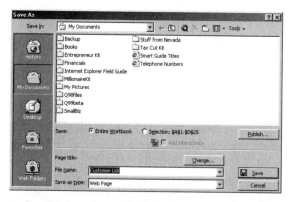

1 Specify where the workbook file should be placed by either clicking the short-cut icons—**History, My Documents, Desktop, Favorites,** or **Web Folders**—or selecting a location from the Save In drop-down list box.

2 Click a Save option button—Entire Workbook or Selection—to specify what you want to save as a web page.

3 Click Change to display a dialog box you can use to give the web page a name.

4 Enter a filename for the new web page in the File Name drop-down list box.

5 Verify that the Save As Type drop-down list box indicates you're saving a web page.

6 Name the workbook file, but don't enter the file extension. Excel adds this for you because it uses the file extension to identify the file type.

7 To save a simple web page that shows a picture of the workbook, click Publish and follow the step-by-step instructions provided by the Web Post Wizard. To save the entire workbook or workbook selection using the HTML file format, click Save. Note that if you click Publish, you're essentially creating a web page that shows a picture of the workbook or workbook selection. And if you click Save, what you're creating is a complete copy of the workbook or workbook selection—except using the HTML file format instead of the traditional binary file format. If you want users to be able to work with your worksheet while in Internet Explorer using **Web Components,** select the Add Interactivity check box.

SEE ALSO   **Save Options; Saving Workbooks**

Saving Workbooks

To save workbooks and the worksheets and charts they contain, choose either the File menu's Save or Save As commands. Or you can also click the Save toolbar button.

Resaving a Workbook

Choose the File menu's Save command or click the Save toolbar button when you have saved the workbook before and want to save the workbook using the same name and in the same location.

Saving a Workbook for the First Time

Choose the File menu's Save As command or click the Save toolbar button when you have created a new workbook and haven't yet saved it.

1 Specify where the workbook file should be placed by either clicking the shortcut icons—History, My Documents, Desktop, Favorites, or Web Folders—or selecting a location from the Save In drop-down list box.

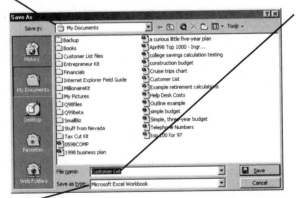

2 Name the workbook file, but don't enter the file extension. Excel adds this for you because it uses the file extension to identify the file type.

3 Select a file type from the Save As Type drop-down list box to save the file in a format other than the usual Excel workbook file format. (Do this, for example, to use the workbook file with another spreadsheet program.)

SEE ALSO   File Properties; Opening Workbooks; Save Options

Scenarios

When you boil it down, a scenario is a collection of values or inputs for specified cells. All you do is store a set of inputs and give the set a name by choosing the Tools menu's Scenarios command. When you want to reuse the inputs, choose Scenarios to indicate which set of inputs you want to use. In effect, then, you get to change many inputs at once by choosing a command rather than by having to individually change values in cells.

Scientific Notation

If a cell uses the General number format, Excel uses scientific notation to display values that are too big or too small to fit neatly within the cell's width.

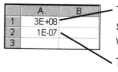

The value 300,000,000 is too big to fit neatly into the standard-width cell, so Excel displays this value as 3E+08, which is equivalent to 3.00×10^8.

The value 0.0000001 is too small to fit neatly into the standard-width cell, so Excel displays this value as 1E-07, which is equivalent to 1.00×10^{-7}.

If a value is very large or very small, Excel may even store a value in the cell that uses scientific notation. For example, suppose you typed the digit 3 followed by 21 zeroes:

3000000000000000000000

Because this value is so large, Excel uses the scientific notation, 3E+21, both for storing and for displaying the value.

Entering values with scientific notation

You can use scientific notation to enter values in cells, too. Although Excel uses an uppercase letter E for scientific notation, you can type either an uppercase E or a lowercase e.

SEE ALSO   Entering Data; Formatting Numbers

Searching Lists

To search a list, follow these steps:

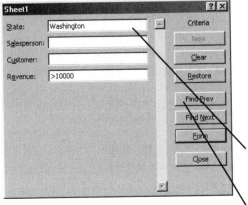

1 Select the list (including the column headings, or headers).

2 Choose the Data menu's Form command.

3 Click Criteria. Excel displays the criteria entry version of the Data Form dialog box.

4 Enter search information in the text boxes to describe the list entry you want to find.

5 Click Find Prev and Find Next to search backward and forward in a list.

If you enter search information in the text boxes, Excel looks for an entry that exactly matches what you enter.

You can also search for values based on a conditional, or **Boolean algebra**, test. Here, for example, the criterion >10000 says to find clients providing more than $10,000 of revenue.

All the criteria you enter are used in the search. By entering both a State and a Revenue criterion, as shown here, Excel looks only for California clients providing more than $10,000 of revenue. Note that you don't have to enter the header, or field, name.

When Excel finds a list entry matching your criteria, it displays the list entry in the Data Form dialog box. To continue looking through the list, click Find Prev and Find Next. To return to the criteria entry version of the Data Form dialog box—perhaps to specify some new criteria—click Criteria.

SEE ALSO   Creating Lists; Sorting Lists

Selecting Cells

You select single cells by clicking and dragging with the mouse or by pressing the direction keys. (The cell you select is called the **active cell.**)

Selecting a Single Cell

Click the cell, or press the direction keys to move the cell selector to the cell.

Selecting Rectangular Ranges of Cells

You can select more than one cell—what's called a "range"—by dragging the mouse between opposite corners of the range. Or you can select a cell, hold down Shift, and then press the direction keys to select a rectangle of cells. (In a range selection, one cell will still be the active cell.)

Selecting Multiple Ranges of Cells

You can also select discontinuous rectangles of cells by holding down Ctrl and then dragging the mouse between the opposite corners of each range.

Selecting the Worksheet

You can select an entire worksheet by clicking the Select All button, which is the blank button that appears in the upper left corner of the workbook document window.

Selecting Columns

You select a column by clicking the column letter label. You select a range of columns by clicking the first column and dragging the mouse to the last column.

Selecting Rows

You select a single row by clicking the row number label. You select a range of rows by clicking the first row and dragging the mouse to the last row.

Sharing Microsoft Excel Data

You can easily share **values, labels, formulas, worksheet ranges, and charts** created in Excel with other Windows-based programs. To share the data, follow these steps:

1 Select what you want to share: a worksheet range, a chart, some formula fragment, or anything else.

2 Choose the Edit menu's Copy command.

3 Switch to the other application by clicking a Taskbar button.

4 Display the document in which you want to place the Excel information.

5 Paste the contents of the Clipboard into the other application's document. (Probably you'll do so with that application's Edit menu's Paste command.)

Linked vs. embedded objects

When Windows pastes an object—a worksheet fragment, for example—into another application's document, you'll usually have a choice as to whether the pasted object is linked to the source document or is merely an embedded copy of the source document. Choose the Edit menu's Paste Special command to make your choice.

SEE ALSO   Clipboard; Switching Tasks

Sheet Page Setup

Choose the File menu's Page Setup command and click the Sheet tab to display the dialog box you use to specify how worksheets should appear on printed pages. (The active sheet must display a worksheet for this tab to appear.)

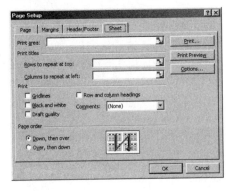

1 Limit the printed portion of the worksheet to a range, such as A1:G3, in the Print Area text box. To specify multiple ranges, place commas between the individual ranges, for example, A1:G30, A35:G75.

2 Indicate whether each printed worksheet page should show a column or a row or a set of columns or rows in the Print Titles text boxes. Do this if you've used rows or columns to hold headings that you want to appear on each page.

3 Select Print check boxes to indicate whether worksheet gridlines, cell comments, and row numbers and column letters, for example, should print.

4 Select a Page Order option to indicate the order in which Excel should print the page-size portions of a worksheet that takes more than a single page to print.

Sheets

Sheets are the pages of a workbook that Excel uses to show **worksheets, chart sheets,** and in rare circumstances, macro sheets, **Visual Basic** modules, and dialog sheets.

Shortcut Menus

Excel knows which commands make sense in which situations. It also knows which commands you, as an Excel user, are most likely to use. If you want, Excel will display a menu of these commands—called the "shortcut menu." All you need to do is point to whatever you want to work with, and click the right button on the mouse.

Solver

Excel provides a Solver add-in that lets you perform optimization modeling, including linear programming. To install the Solver add-in, choose the Tools menu's Add-Ins command, select the Solver check box, and then press Enter. (When you do this, Excel installs the Solver add-in.) After you've installed the Solver add-in, Excel adds the Solver command to the Tools menu.

SEE ALSO **Goal Seek**

Sorting Lists

If you've defined a list using the Data menu's Form command, you can sort the entries alphabetically based on a field that stores labels or in ascending or descending order based on a field that stores a value. To sort a list, follow these steps:

1 Select the list entries.

2 Choose the Data menu's Sort command. Excel displays the Sort dialog box.

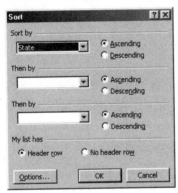

3 Name the field used for alphabetizing or ordering in the Sort By drop-down list box.

4 Select a Sort By option to indicate whether you want alphabetic list entries arranged in A to Z or Z to A order, or whether you want value list entries arranged in ascending or descending order.

5 Add second and third sorting keys in the Then By drop-down list boxes, and then select Then By options.

6 Select a My List Has option to indicate whether the first selected row names the fields.

The Sort tools

You can use the Sort tools to arrange the selected list entries in either ascending or descending order based on the first field.

SEE ALSO   **Creating Lists**

Spelling

You can choose the Tools menu's Spelling command or click the Spelling toolbar button to check the spelling of words used in **labels.** To use the command or toolbar button, first select the worksheet area you want to spell-check (if you're interested in checking only a limited area). Then choose the command, or click the button. Excel displays the Spelling dialog box, alerting you to words it can't find in its dictionary. Use it to control how Excel spell-checks and what Excel does when it finds a possible error.

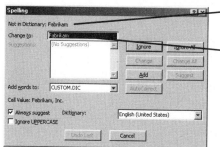

Excel alerts you to words it can't find in its dictionary.

Excel suggests an alternative spelling with the Change To text box if the Always Suggest check box is selected. You can edit whatever Excel suggests or select another word from the Suggestions list box.

Using the Spelling Buttons

When Excel finds a potentially misspelled word, click the Spelling buttons to indicate what Excel should do:

Button	What it does
Ignore	Ignore only this occurrence of the word.
Ignore All	Ignore this and every other occurrence of the word.
Change	Change this occurrence of the word to what the Change To text box shows.
Change All	Change this and every other occurrence of the word to what the Change To text box shows.
Add	Add the word to the spelling dictionary named in the Add Words To drop-down list box.
Suggest	Look through the Excel spelling dictionary and the custom dictionary named in the Add Words To drop-down list box for similarly spelled words.
AutoCorrect	Add the misspelled word and its correct spelling to the list of words and phrases that are corrected automatically.

Starting Excel

You start Excel (and other Windows-based programs) either by opening a document (or file) created by the program or by opening the program itself.

Starting Excel by Opening Documents

To start a program by opening a document, follow these steps:

1 Start Windows Explorer.

2 Display the folder with the document.

3 Double-click the document icon.

Starting a Program Directly

To start a program without opening a document, click the Start button, choose Programs, and then choose the program.

About the Documents menu

The Documents menu within the Windows Start menu lists up to 15 of the most recently revised documents. If you see the document you want on this menu—remember this may be an Excel workbook—you can open it by selecting it.

Statistics Functions

A statistics **function** calculates some statistical measure. A special variety of statistics functions—the database functions—even calculate statistical measures of selected values from an Excel list or database.

Here is a sampling of Excel's general statistics functions:

Function	What it does
=AVERAGE(2,3,4,5,1)	Returns the average of the values 2, 3, 4, 5, and 1, which is 3.
=MAX(23,456,12)	Returns the maximum value included as an argument, which is 456.
=STDEV(2,3,2.5,2,2.5,3)	Returns the sample standard deviation of the values included as arguments, which is 0.447214.

The general statistics functions accept a maximum of 30 **arguments**. Arguments don't have to be values or cell addresses, however. Arguments can also reference worksheet ranges. In this way, you can calculate statistical measurements for large samples and populations. (The worksheet range B1:B10000, for example, is a single argument that references 10,000 cells.)

Styles

A style is a combination of formatting choices.

Creating a new style SEE **Adding Styles**

Deleting an existing style SEE **Removing Styles**

Using an existing style SEE **Applying Styles**

Subtotaling Lists

You can use the Data menu's Subtotals command to subtotal columns with values in a list.

Using the Subtotals Command

To use this command, first sort the list using the field you'll subtotal. Then select the list (including the column headings, or header row), and choose the Data menu's Subtotals command. When Excel displays the Subtotal dialog box, follow these steps:

1 Specify where subtotals should be calculated, such as subtotals by state, in the At Each Change In drop-down list box.

continues

135

Subtotaling Lists *(continued)*

2 Select the summary calculation Excel should make from the Use Function drop-down list box. (Usually you sum, but Excel lets you make any statistical calculation: average, maximum, minimum, and so on.)

3 Indicate which columns should have subtotals calculated in the Add Subtotal To drop-down list box.

4 Select check boxes to control where Excel places new subtotal information.

5 Click OK. Excel subtotals the list.

Working with Subtotaled Lists

Using the default check box settings, Excel places subtotal and grand total information beneath the list.

1 2 3		A	B	C	D	E
	1	State	Salesperson	Customer	Revenue	
	2	Washington	Bob	A. Datum Corporation	$ 21,851.18	
	3	Washington	Jose	Adventure Works	$ 97,981.45	
	4	Washington	Marie	Alpine Ski Center	$ 96,920.43	
	5	Washington	Yoshio	Arbor Shoes	$ 76,697.18	
	6	Washington	Bob	Baldwin Museum of Science	$ 64,118.56	
	7	Washington	Jose	Blue Yonder Airways	$ 29,505.58	
	8	**Washington Total**			$ 387,074.38	
	9	Oregon	Marie	City Power and Light	$ 95,458.66	
	10	Oregon	Yoshio	Chateau St. Mark	$ 20,642.24	
	11	Oregon	Bob	Clark Escrow, Inc.	$ 48,548.84	
	12	Oregon	Jose	Coho Vineyard	$ 19,247.76	
	13	Oregon	Marie	Duffy Vineyards	$ 53,366.45	
	14	Oregon	Yoshio	Duluth Mutual Life	$ 33,036.87	
	15	Oregon	Bob	Exotic Excursions	$ 76,251.94	
	16	Oregon	Jose	Fabrikam, Inc.	$ 91,436.39	
	17	**Oregon Total**			$ 437,989.14	
	18	California	Marie	Hanson Brothers	$ 17,916.96	
	19	California	Yoshio	Hav Buv Tovs	$ 83,613.44	

Use the 1, 2, and 3 buttons to tell Excel how much detail it should show in the subtotaled list. The 1 button tells Excel to show only the grand total, 2 tells Excel to show the grand total and any subtotals, and 3 tells Excel to show the individual list entries.

To hide the individual list entries that go into a subtotal, click the Minus button on the left. After Excel hides the list entries that go into a subtotal, it changes the Minus button to a Plus button. Click the Plus button to unhide the list entries.

Subtotaling filtered lists

By subtotaling a filtered list, it's easy to perform many otherwise complicated calculations. You can count the times a particular entry occurs by filtering a list so that it includes only the entries you want to count, for example. And you can tally a value field for a subset of list entries. All you need to do is filter the list so that it shows only the subset.

SEE ALSO AutoSum; Creating Lists; Sorting Lists

Switching Tasks

To multitask, or run multiple programs, in the Windows operating system, you use the Start button and the Taskbar. You click the Start button to start new applications, and you click application buttons on the Taskbar to switch between the applications you've already started.

Tables SEE What-If Tables

Text Boxes

A text box is a box with text that floats over a worksheet or a chart sheet. You can use text boxes effectively to annotate worksheets and charts.

Text Functions

Most **functions** manipulate values, but Excel also provides functions that manipulate text. The textual arguments in a text function can be either addresses of cells containing text labels or text strings enclosed in quotation marks. Here are some sample text functions:

Function	What it does
=PROPER("mr. president")	Capitalizes initial letter of each word in string, returning Mr. President.
=REPT("Walla",2)	Repeats the first argument the number of times specified in the second argument, returning WallaWalla.
=LEN("Chrysanthemum")	Counts the number of characters in a text string, returning 13.

SEE ALSO   **Argument; Text String Formulas**

Text String Formulas

Excel formulas usually manipulate values arithmetically: adding, subtracting, multiplying, dividing, and exponentiating. (This last word doesn't appear in any dictionary, by the way. I just made it up.) You should know, though, that it's also possible to create formulas that manipulate text by combining text labels, extracting blocks of text from a label, and even changing the capitalization of the letters in a label.

To combine text labels—the simplest text string formula—use the concatenation operator, &. With the concatenation operator, you can string together two or more pieces of text—including blanks. Here are some examples of text string concatenation formulas. Note that the second and third examples enter a space character between the two words by including a blank character in quotation marks. Note that the third example assumes that cell A1 holds the label Dashiell and that cell A2 holds the label Hammett.

Formula	What it returns
="Walla"&"Walla"	WallaWalla
="Raymond"&" "&"Chandler"	Raymond Chandler
=A1&" "&A2	Dashiell Hammett

For other text string formulas, you'll need to use Excel's **text functions**.

Time Formats

Excel provides eight time formats that you can use to make **time values** understandable. To format a time, select the cell or range with the time values. Then choose the Format menu's Cells command, and select Time from the Category list box. Finally, select one of the time formats from the Type list box.

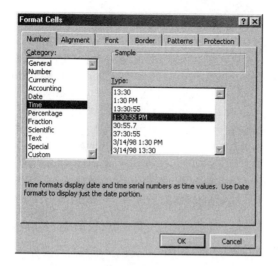

SEE ALSO   Date Formats; Formatting Numbers

Time Functions SEE Date and Time Functions

Time Values

Excel lets you use decimal values to represent times: 0 represents 12:00 AM, 0.25 represents 6:00 AM, 0.5 represents 12:00 PM, and so forth. Time values let you easily perform arithmetic using times. For example, you can calculate the number of hours someone works if that person starts at 6:00 AM and works until 3:30 PM.

Date and time combinations

Combine date integer values with time decimal values to show both the date and the time. For example, to represent 12:00 PM on July 6, 2009, you use the value 40000.5. The integer portion of the value, 40000, is the date value for July 6, 2009. The decimal portion of the value, 0.5, is the time value for 12:00 PM.

SEE ALSO   Date and Time Functions; Formulas; Time Formats

Toolbars

Toolbars are those rows of buttons and boxes that appear at the top of your window just below the menu bar. Past versions of Excel displayed two toolbars: the Standard toolbar and the Formatting toolbar. The current version of Excel displays a single Personal toolbar in place of the Standard and Formatting toolbars. Excel initially places only the Personal toolbar in its application window. But Excel also provides several other toolbars.

Adding and Removing Toolbars

To add or remove any of the toolbars, point to the toolbar, click the right mouse button, and then—when Excel displays a list of the available toolbars—click the one you want. (Or choose the View menu's Toolbars command to accomplish the same thing.)

Toolbar button names

When you place the cursor on a toolbar button, Excel displays the button name in a tiny yellow box, called a "ScreenTip."

SEE ALSO **Personal Menus and Toolbars; Quick Reference: Toolbar Button Guide**

Underline Characters

You can underline selected characters in the current worksheet selection by pressing Ctrl+U or clicking the Underline toolbar button. You can also choose the Format menu's Cells command and select its Font tab options.

SEE ALSO **Changing Fonts**

Undo

You can usually undo your last change to a workbook by choosing the Edit menu's Undo command or by clicking the Undo toolbar button.

After you choose the Undo command or click the Undo toolbar button, Excel enables the Redo command. Choose the Edit menu's Redo command to undo the effect of choosing Undo.

Irreversible damage

The Undo command undoes workbook changes made with the Edit, Insert, and Format menu commands and some changes made with the Data menu commands. The command also undoes workbook changes made by entering or editing data in cells. The Undo command doesn't undo all workbook changes, however. For example, you can't undo workbook changes made with File menu commands.

Unicode

Unicode refers to an encoding standard that lets computers work with practically any character—Roman, Hebrew, Thai, Japanese, and so on—used on a computer. Unicode therefore works with most of the languages in the world. It also works with just about any mathematical or technical symbols you will see. Microsoft Office 2000 programs, including Excel, support the Unicode standard.

URL

The URL, or uniform resource locator, specifies how you find an Internet resource such as a **World Wide Web** page. A URL has four parts: the service, or protocol; the server name; the path; and the document, or file, name.

A Sample URL Explained

Let me explain each of these parts, using a real-life Web page—the one that provides biographical data on the President of the United States and his family.

`http://www.whitehouse.gov/White_House/html/Life.html`

`http://` identifies this resource as part of the World Wide Web.

`www.whitehouse.gov/` identifies the server.

`White_House/html/` names the directory and subdirectory of the World Wide Web document.

`Life.html` names the World Wide Web document.

Validation

You can tell Excel that it should validate, or double-check, any inputs you enter into cells. To do this, select the cell or range for which you want to validate input. Then choose the Data menu's Validation command. When Excel displays the Data Validation dialog box, click the Settings tab. Next, select the validation rule you want to use from the Allow list box. Then use the other text boxes that Excel displays to describe how the validation rule should be applied.

The Data Validation dialog box also provides two other tabs useful for working with data validation. You can use the Input Message tab to describe an input instruction message you want people to see if they select the cell. And you can use the Error Alert tab to describe an error message you want people to see if they attempt to enter data that fails the validation rule.

Values

A value is a number you enter in a cell that you want to later use in a formula. In general, a value can include the numbers 1, 2, 3, 4, 5, 6, 7, 8, 9, and 0 and the period symbol to indicate a decimal point, if needed. You can also include numeric formatting with a value—for example, currency symbols and commas—if you want Excel to use the formatting to display the value. If you want to enter a negative value, precede the number with a hyphen or enclose it in parentheses.

SEE ALSO   **Entering Data; Formatting Numbers; Labels; Scientific Notation**

Views

You can tell Excel to remember the way a worksheet appears in the workbook window: its size, position, displayed area, and so on.

Creating a View

To create a view, choose the View menu's Custom Views command and then click Add. When Excel displays the Add View dialog box, Name the view in the Name text box.

Using a View

To see the view, choose the View menu's Custom Views command, select the view, and then click Show.

Visual Basic

Visual Basic is Excel's built-in programming language. Visual Basic is very useful, but it's really a development tool for people with programming experience. For this reason, most users won't have occasion to work with the tool. Note, however, that most people can create and use powerful macros as a way to automate Excel tasks.

Web Components

Microsoft Office 2000 includes three small programs called Web Components that run inside Microsoft Internet Explorer. You use them to view and manipulate Excel and Microsoft Access data published on a web site. You use the Spreadsheet, PivotTable, and Chart components in almost the same way you use Excel. To interact with data on the Web using a Web Component, you need to have an Office 2000 program installed on your computer and be using Internet Explorer 4.01 or later.

To create a web page using Web Components that allow users to interact with your data, choose the File menu's Save As Web page command. Click Publish, select the Add Interactivity With check box, and select which Web Component is most appropriate for your data. Click Publish when you're finished.

Web Folder

The Web Folder shortcut icon, which appears on the Open, Save, and Save As Web Page dialog boxes, lists web server locations you can use for storing and retrieving Excel workbooks.

SEE ALSO   Opening Workbooks; Saving Web Pages; Saving Workbooks

Web Page Preview

You can preview how an Excel workbook will look as a web page using your default web browser. To do so, choose the File menu's Web Page Preview command.

SEE ALSO   Saving Web Pages

Web Query

Excel supplies a web query command you can use to extract information stored in web pages and then place this information in a workbook. To use this feature, follow these steps:

1 Choose the Data menu's Get External Data command, and then choose the submenu's New Web Query command. Excel displays the New Web Query dialog box.

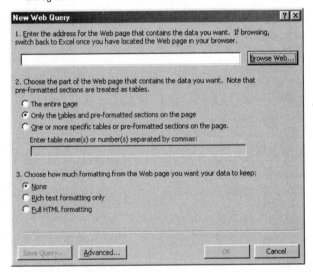

2 Enter the full **URL** for the web page in the text box provided. You can also enter a regular Windows **pathname**.

3 Select an option from the first set of option buttons to indicate what portion of the web page you want to query. If you indicate that you want to query only specific tables on the page, name the tables in the text box provided.

4 Optionally, select an option from the second set of option buttons to specify which formatting you want Excel to apply.

5 Click OK to query the page. Excel extracts the web page data, placing it in a workbook.

What-If Tables

What-if tables show a series of calculations using the same formula but a different value for each calculation. You might use a what-if table, for example, to forecast the different future value amounts you accumulate in a retirement account based on different annual contributions.

Creating a What-If Table

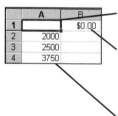

Leave an input cell at the left corner of the what-if table; Excel needs this for the calculations.

Enter the what-if formula next to the input cell. The formula should reference the empty cell and any other needed inputs. This formula, for example, uses the future value function =FV(0.1,35,-A1).

Enter the input values for the what-if calculations in the column beneath the input cell.

Performing What-If Analysis

After you've set up the what-if table, follow these steps:

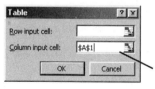

1 Select the what-if table.

2 Choose the Data menu's Table command. Excel displays the Table dialog box.

3 Identify the what-if input cell in the Column Input Cell text box.

continues

145

What-If Tables *(continued)*

	A	B
1		$0.00
2	2000	542048.7
3	2500	677560.9
4	3750	1016341

Excel uses the what-if formula to calculate results for each of the input values and then places these values in the cells beneath the what-if formula.

The future value amount accumulated based on a $2,000-a-year contribution, a 10 percent annual return, and 35 years of contributions is $542,048.74.

Table recalculation

Excel uses a special **function,** =TABLE(), to calculate the what-if formula values. If you change an input, Excel recalculates the what-if table value that uses the input. For example, if you want to see the future value amount accumulated based on a $5,000-a-year contribution, change the value in cell A4 to 5000.

SEE ALSO   Goal Seek

Window Panes

If you use rows to label columns or columns to label rows, you may want these rows and columns to stay visible—even when you scroll up and down and left and right in a worksheet. To fix the placement of labeling rows and columns, turn the labeling rows and columns into "panes." Then freeze the panes.

Creating Window Panes

Position the **cell selector** at the cell below the row and to the right of the column you want to use as panes. Then choose the Window menu's Split command.

Freezing Window Panes

To freeze—or to simultaneously create and freeze the panes—so that they label columns and rows even as you scroll down and to the right, choose the Window menu's Freeze Panes command.

Removing Window Panes

To remove a window pane, choose the Window menu's Remove Split command. (This command replaces the Split command after you've split a window into panes.)

Unfreezing Window Panes

To unfreeze a window pane, choose the Window menu's Unfreeze Panes command. (This command replaces the Freeze Panes command after you've frozen a window's panes.)

Jumping between window panes

You can move the cell selector between window panes by pressing F6.

Word

You can use Excel worksheets and charts in your Microsoft Word documents. In fact, because Excel's worksheets are more powerful than Word's tables and because Excel's charts are more powerful than those available within Word, you'll find that it's often a good idea to do this.

To use an Excel worksheet selection or Excel chart in a Word document, first select the worksheet range or chart. Next, choose the Excel Edit menu's Copy command. Then, switch to Word, position the insertion point where you want the worksheet or chart, and choose the Word Edit menu's Paste command.

SEE ALSO   Switching Tasks

Workbook Functions

Workbook functions return information about a workbook, your computer, or the operating environment. For example, the following **function** tells Excel to retrieve information about the operating system:

=INFO(osversion)

If you're using Windows 98, this function returns the string "Windows (32 bit) 4.10."

SEE ALSO   Argument

Workbooks

Excel arranges **worksheets** and **chart sheets** into stacks of sheets—analogous to a pad of spreadsheet paper. Excel calls these stacked sheets workbooks; and it stores workbooks as files on disk.

SEE ALSO New Workbooks; Opening Workbooks; Saving Workbooks

Worksheet Pictures SEE Pictures

Worksheets

An Excel **workbook** consists of worksheets and **chart sheets.** A worksheet is the on-screen spreadsheet. Organized into rows and columns, it lets you easily build tables of **labels, values,** and **formulas.**

Worksheet Titles

Worksheet titles is a Lotus 1-2-3 term. It refers to rows you fix because they label columns and columns you fix because they label rows. (By "fix," I mean you don't want them scrolled when you scroll down and to the right in the worksheet.) Excel doesn't use worksheet titles. Excel does, however, provide **window panes,** which let you accomplish the same thing.

Worksheet Views

You can control the appearance of the worksheet. To do so, choose the Tools menu's Options command, click the View tab, and then make your changes.

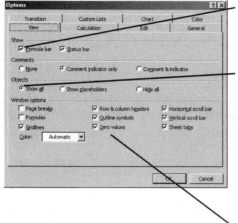

Select the Show check boxes to indicate whether you want the formula bar and status bar to appear.

Select one of the Objects options to indicate how worksheet objects should appear: Show All displays the object, Show Placeholders tells Excel to display a gray rectangle in place of the object, And Hide All hides the object and displays no placeholder.

Select the Window Options check boxes to control whether worksheets show, for example, automatic page breaks, formulas (instead of the usual formula results), and gridlines.

Workspace

A workspace is a list of workbooks. You can save a workspace, or workbook list, by choosing the File menu's Save Workspace command—in which case, you save each of the open workbooks and the list of the open workbooks. To later reopen each of the workbooks listed in the workspace, open the workspace. Saving a workspace works just like saving a workbook. By the way, workspace files have the extension .xlw.

SEE ALSO   Save Options; Saving Workbooks

World Wide Web

The World Wide Web (also known as WWW, or simply the Web) is a set of multimedia documents that are connected so that you can jump from one document to another using **hyperlinks,** usually with just a click of the mouse. The multimedia part means that you're not limited to words: you can place pictures, sounds, and even video clips in a web document.

continues

World Wide Web *(continued)*

To view a World Wide Web document, you need to have a web browser. Popular web browsers include Netscape Navigator, Mosaic, and Microsoft Internet Explorer. (Excel now comes with its own web browser, so you don't really need another.)

If you want to start exploring the Web, try using a searching tool such as Yahoo! You can find it at the **URL** address *http:// www.yahoo.com.* Yahoo! provides a directory of thousands of different World Wide Web sites.

Year 2000

Excel doesn't present any of the year 2000 problems you might be hearing about. Excel uses four-digit year numbers, so it recognizes dates through December 31, 9999.

Troubleshooting

Got a problem? Starting on
the next page are solutions
to the problems that sometimes plague new users of
Microsoft Excel. You'll be
on your way—and safely
out of trouble—in no time.

Cell Entries

You Can't Show Long Labels

A label that is longer than a cell is wide won't fit in the cell. Microsoft Excel, however, has several ways to fix this.

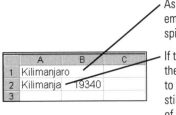

As long as the cell immediately to the right is empty, Excel lets the long label, Kilimanjaro, spill over.

If the neighboring cell contains data, however, the displayed label, Kilimanjaro, is truncated to fit the width of the cell. Although the cell still holds the entire long label, only a portion of the label is displayed.

You can deal with cutoff labels in several ways.

Shorten the label

You can shorten the label by editing it, for example. (Perhaps all you need to do is abbreviate a word.)

Use smaller characters

1 Choose the Format menu's Cells command.

2 Click the Font tab option for font and point-size changes.

Using Detect And Repair

If you see that Excel is displaying cell contents using the wrong **font**, it may be that a font file became corrupted. In this case, choose the Help menu's **Detect And Repair** command. Detect And Repair fixes noncritical files such as font files.

Increase the column width

This is easy—choose the Format menu's Column, AutoFit command.

▶ Split the label into separate lines

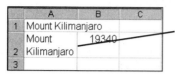

1 Choose the Format menu's Cells command.

2 Click the Alignment tab, and select Justify from the Vertical Text Alignment drop-down list box so that Excel splits the label into separate lines.

SEE ALSO Aligning Labels and Values; Columns; Rows

You Can't Show a Value Except as #####

If a cell isn't wide enough to display a value, Excel shows a series of # symbols. In the worksheet fragment below, the value I've entered, 1000000 is too wide for the cell.

In the following cells, though, I've made formatting changes, so the value fits.

▶ Increase the column width

Choose the Format menu's Column, AutoFit command.

▶ Use smaller characters

1 Choose the Format menu's Cells command.

2 Select the Font tab option for font and point-size changes.

3 Select a condensed font, if available.

4 Select a smaller point size, if appropriate.

▶ Format the number with fewer punctuation characters: commas, currency symbols, decimal places, and so on

This is just a matter of selecting a number format that uses fewer punctuation characters.

If you're using currency symbols and commas, for example, switching to a format that uses only commas will save a single character, the dollar sign.

continues

You Can't Show a Value Except as ##### *(continued)*

If you're working with two decimal places and switch to a format with zero decimal places, you'll save three characters: the two decimal places and the decimal point.

▶ Use the General number format

The General number format converts values that are too wide to **scientific notation.** To use the General number format, follow these steps:

1 Select the worksheet range with the cells you want to reformat.

2 Choose the Format menu's Cells command.

3 Click the Number tab.

4 Select General from the Category list box.

SEE ALSO Columns; Formatting Numbers; Rows

You Can't Enter a Label

If you try to enter a **label** that looks like a **value,** Excel may enter what you type as a value—not as a label. In the example below, Excel would read the part numbers as dates.

▶ Add a label prefix

You can force Excel to accept a cell entry as a label, however, by typing an apostrophe and then the label.

In the figure below, check out the entry "12-8-93" in the formula bar. It's preceded by an apostrophe—which you can barely see, so look carefully. That tells Excel that this is a label and not a value.

| A2 | ▼ | = | '12-8-93 |

	A	B	C
1	Part No	Part Description	Quantity
2	12-8-93	8-foot Cedar 1x4's	350
3	12-12-93	12-foot Cedar 1x4's	350

▶ Use the text function

If you don't want to include a label prefix, you can also use the **text function.** Use the **Function** command to build the Text function.

In using the text function, you'll need to provide the value that you really want entered as a label and a number format, which should be used to format the value before it becomes a label. (If you don't know which number you want, simply specify the General format.)

You Can't Enter Anything in a Cell

If you want to enter something into a cell but Excel won't let you, then someone has told Excel to lock its cells—which probably means you're not supposed to be entering data in the cell.

Unlock the cell protection

If you're sure you should be entering data in a locked cell, you can unlock, or unprotect, the cell. To do this, choose the Tools menu's Protection, Unprotect Sheet command. Excel may prompt you for a password if whoever locked the cells assigned a password. You'll need to give this password to Excel.

SEE ALSO Cell Protection

Calculating Formulas

You Can't Get a Work- book to Calculate

If you've set a workbook to manual recalculation (or someone in your office has—perhaps without your knowledge), you'll need to tell Excel when it should recalculate workbooks. Fortunately, Excel will tell you whenever it thinks you should consider recalculating.

Ready   Calculate — The status bar shows the word *Calculate* whenever a workbook needs to be recalculated.

Manually force recalculation
To recalculate the workbook, press F9.

Make worksheet calculation automatic
To tell Excel it should automatically recalculate a workbook, choose the Tools menu's Option command, and then click the Calculation tab.

continues

You Can't Get a Workbook to Calculate *(continued)*

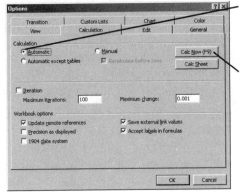

Select the Automatic option. Now Excel will recalculate formulas any time their inputs change.

You can also recalculate the workbook by clicking Calc Now. It works just like pressing F9.

Calculating a single cell

You can tell Excel to calculate the formula in a single cell by double-clicking the cell and then pressing Enter. Note, however, that if the cell's formula depends on the results of other formulas, these other formulas don't get recalculated. They may need to be recalculated, however, if their inputs have changed.

Excel Doesn't Recognize Your Entry as a Formula

If Excel looks at the **formula** you enter but doesn't think it's a formula, you've forgotten to start the formula with an arithmetic operator such as the equal sign (=).

Edit the formula

Simply edit the formula so that it starts with an equal or plus sign.

You Can't Correctly Calculate a Formula

Even if **formula** results seem wrong, Excel is calculating the formula correctly. The problem is that the formula you've entered isn't actually the one you want to calculate. Your problem really boils down to one of operator precedence.

Override the standard operator precedence

To force Excel to calculate in the order you want, enclose the first calculation you want made in parentheses. Then enclose the second calculation you want made in parentheses. Then the third calculation, and so on.

A Financial Function Doesn't Work Correctly

Excel's **financial functions** are extremely powerful, but they're sometimes hard to use. Excel requires the function **arguments** to follow a very specific set of rules. If you can't get a financial function to calculate correctly, your situation is most likely a problem with one of the arguments.

 Use a decimal interest rate

The interest argument that most of the financial functions use is a decimal value. The interest rate 8 percent, for example, is actually the decimal value 0.08. One of the more common mistakes new users of Excel make is entering this decimal value as an integer such as 8. If you enter 8 instead of 0.08, you've actually specified the interest rate as 800 percent and not as 8 percent.

 Use a periodic interest rate

Another common problem with interest rate arguments is not using the correct periodic rate; for example, using an annual interest rate in a monthly loan payment **formula.** The payment periods—such as months—must agree with the interest rate periods. If you're calculating a monthly loan payment, you need to use a monthly interest rate. If you're calculating the principal balance on a loan with quarterly payments, you need to use a quarterly interest rate. If you're calculating the future value accumulated in a bimonthly savings plan, you must use a bimonthly interest rate.

Converting annual interest rates

In almost all cases, you can convert an annual interest rate to a periodic interest rate by dividing the annual interest rate by the number of periods in a year. For example, because there are 12 months in a year, if the annual interest rate is 6 percent, you can calculate the monthly interest rate by dividing 6 percent by 12, for a result of 0.5 percent.

continues

A Financial Function Doesn't Work Correctly *(continued)*

Differentiate cash inflows and outflows with signs

One other quirky but quite logical aspect of Excel's financial function set is that it requires you to differentiate cash inflows and outflows: Money you pay out needs to be included as a negative value, and money you receive needs to be included as a positive value. You indicate negative argument values with a minus sign.

This sounds complicated, but really it's not. Take the case of a loan payment calculation made with the loan payment function. The dollar amount included as a loan balance amount is a positive amount (because you receive the loan from the lender), and the payment amount, calculated by the function in this case, is a negative value (because you will pay out the loan payment).

Here's another example. Suppose you will save $2,000 a year and want to estimate the future value you accumulate using the Future Value function. In this case, the $2,000 payment argument is a negative value (because you pay out this amount), and the future value amount returned by the function is a positive amount (because you will receive this amount at some point in the future).

Menus and Toolbars

Your Menu Commands Disappear

Excel has a new feature—Personal Menus. When you first start working with the program, it keeps track of those menu commands you use and don't use, and it automatically customizes your menus. It's a pretty cool feature; because the menu's shorter, it's easier to access the commands you use most.

However, it can be a bit disconcerting when commands just up and vanish.

Find the missing commands

They're not really gone, just hiding. To use one of the hidden commands, just rest your cursor on the menu title for a moment and the full list of commands will pop up.

If it doesn't, choose the Tools menu's Customize command, click the Options tab, and make sure the Show Full Menus After A Short Delay check box is selected.

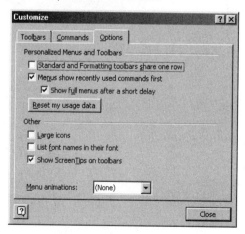

 Reset your menus and toolbars

You can also reset your menus and toolbars to the original configuration by clicking Reset My Usage Data. Excel will start learning your preferences all over again.

Your Toolbar Buttons Appear or Disappear

Along with Personal Menus, Excel has Personal Toolbars. The program customizes your toolbar to with the buttons you use most.

Find your missing buttons

Click the little double-chevron button on the toolbar. Since there are usually two toolbars (Standard and Formatting) displayed, you might find two double-chevron buttons.

 —— Your missing buttons pop up in a toolbar extension.

Customize the toolbar manually

If you want to manually control what's on your toolbar, choose Add Or Remove Buttons on the toolbar extension. Or choose the Tools menu's Customize command, click the Commands tab, and drag buttons to and from the toolbars to suit your needs.

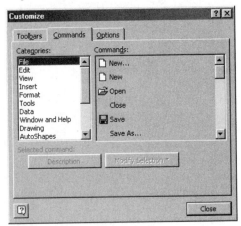

Printing

You Can't Fit Something on a Printed Page (or Two)

Let's say you've got something that you want to fit on a single printed page—or even a couple of pages. Unfortunately, the print area is a bit too large. You have two options for dealing with this problem.

Change the worksheet dimensions

You can make a worksheet smaller by using shorter rows and narrower columns. Choose the Format menu's Row command to shorten row heights. Choose the Format menu's Column command to narrow columns. Note that you may have problems with labels getting cut off and values getting displayed as a series of # symbols when you shorten and narrow the columns.

Reduce the printed size

If you don't want to change the screen size of a worksheet but only its printed size, you can tell Excel to fit a worksheet (or set of worksheets) on a specified number of pages.

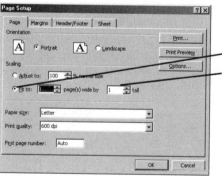

1 Choose the File menu's Page Setup command, and click the Page tab.

2 Click the Fit To option button.

3 Enter amounts in the Fit To text boxes to indicate how many pages wide by how many pages tall Excel should print.

4 Click Print. Excel prints the worksheet on the specified number of pages by reducing the worksheet size. With a little luck, you'll still be able to read what Excel prints.

Previewing pages

Remember, to see what your printed pages will look like, click the File menu's Print Preview command.

SEE ALSO Printing

You Can't Tell Where Excel Breaks Pages

Excel automatically breaks a big worksheet into page-size portions. You may want to see where these page breaks will occur before the actual printing.

▶ **Print Preview a workbook**

Choose the File menu's Print Preview command, and then close the Print Preview window.

34 Rochester	25,254	25,222	25,238	23,219	24,644
35 San Diego	44,376	45,232	44,804	41,220	42,645
36 San Francisco	873,738	800,432	837,085	770,118	774,543
37 San Luis Obispo	90,210	77,324	83,767	77,066	78,491
38 Santa Fe	43,556	67,543	55,550	51,106	52,531
39 Seattle	6,432	5,554	5,993	5,514	6,939

After Excel breaks a worksheet into page-size portions, vertical and horizontal page breaks display as dashed lines.

SEE ALSO Print Preview

You Want to Cancel a Printing Workbook

If you've told Excel to print a workbook that you later realize you don't want to print, you may want to cancel the **printing**. This is particularly true if the workbook requires many pages to print.

▶ **Delete the print job**

When Excel prints a workbook, it creates a print spool file that it sends to Microsoft Windows. Windows then prints this print spool file as well as any other spool files that Excel and other applications have sent. To cancel a printing Excel workbook, follow these steps:

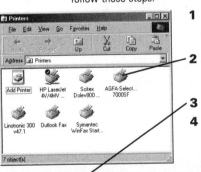

1 Click the Start button, choose Settings, and then choose Printers to display the Printers window.

2 Double-click the printer icon for the printer you're using to display the print queue for the printer.

3 Click the printing Excel workbook.

4 Press Delete, or choose the Document menu's Cancel Printing command.

SEE ALSO Switching Tasks

Files

You Can't Remember Your Password

If you or someone else assigned a password to open a workbook file, you'll need to supply that password before you open the file. If you forget your password or can't seem to enter it correctly, Excel won't let you open the workbook.

 ### Try a password with different-case letters

Excel differentiates passwords on the basis of the letter-case. The following words, for example, are all different passwords from Excel's point of view: Wathers, wATHERS, and WATHERS. For this reason, if you think you know the password, try changing the lowercase letters to uppercase letters and vice versa. It may be that you entered the password with a different combination of uppercase and lowercase letters than you think. (This can occur, for instance, if you happened to press Caps Lock before entering the password.)

SEE ALSO Opening Workbooks; Save Options; Saving Workbooks

You Can't Find a File

Large hard disks make it easy to misplace a file. Fortunately, Windows provides an extremely powerful tool for finding lost files, the Find File feature. Because Excel workbooks are files, you can use Find File to locate lost workbooks.

Because Find File is so powerful and tremendously useful, I'm going to describe it in detail here.

 ### Use Find File

To start Find File, click the Start button, choose Find, and then choose Files Or Folders. Windows displays the Find: All Files dialog box.

continues

You Can't Find a File *(continued)*

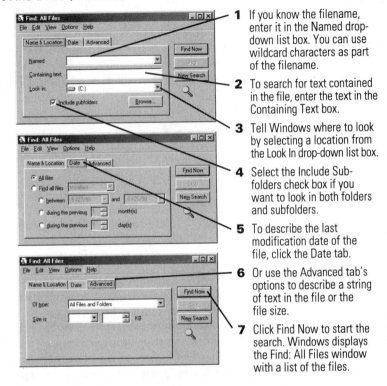

1 If you know the filename, enter it in the Named drop-down list box. You can use wildcard characters as part of the filename.

2 To search for text contained in the file, enter the text in the Containing Text box.

3 Tell Windows where to look by selecting a location from the Look In drop-down list box.

4 Select the Include Sub-folders check box if you want to look in both folders and subfolders.

5 To describe the last modification date of the file, click the Date tab.

6 Or use the Advanced tab's options to describe a string of text in the file or the file size.

7 Click Find Now to start the search. Windows displays the Find: All Files window with a list of the files.

If you accidentally erase a file

To restore a file you've deleted, double-click the Recycle Bin icon to display the Recycle Bin window. Then, select the file you want to restore and choose the File menu's Restore command.

Error Messages

Excel Gives You an Error Message or Behaves Oddly

Excel is a large, complex program. Sometimes files get corrupted, which can adversely affect its performance.

 Run Detect And Repair

Choose the Help menu's Detect And Repair command to fix noncritical files, such as font files.

Quick Reference

Any time you explore a new
program, you're bound to
see features and tools you
can't identify. To be sure
you can identify the
commands and toolbar
buttons you see in
Microsoft Excel, this
Quick Reference
describes these items in
systematic detail.

Worksheet Menu Guide

File Menu

New...	Opens a new, blank workbook.
Open...	Retrieves an existing workbook or workspace from disk.
Close	Removes the active workbook's window from the screen.
Save	Resaves the active workbook as long as you've already saved it once before.
Save **A**s...	Saves a workbook the first time or under a different name.
Save As Web Page...	Saves a worksheet or entire workbook as an HTML document you can publish on an Internet web site.
Save **W**orkspace...	Saves all the open workbooks and also creates a list of open workbooks.
We**b** Page Preview	Displays a window showing how the workbook will look as web pages.
Page Set**u**p...	Allows you to set page size, orientation, margins, headers and footers, and other layout options.
Prin**t** Area	Displays the Print Area submenu.
	Set Print Area Tells Excel to print the selected worksheet range whenever you choose the File Print command.
	Clear Print Area Removes the print area specified by the Set Print Area command.
Print Pre**v**iew	Displays a window showing how printed workbook pages will look.
Print...	Prints the active workbook.
Sen**d** To	Displays the Send To submenu.
	Mail Recipient Sends the current Excel workbook in an e-mail message to the recipient(s) you choose.
	M**a**il Recipient (As Attachment)... Sends the current Excel workbook to the recipient(s) you choose as an attachment to an e-mail message.

Routing Recipient... Sends the current Excel workbook to a group of e-mail recipients and allows you to specify whether it is sent to them sequentially or all at once.

Exchange Folder... Sends the current workbook to a folder in your Microsoft Exchange client mailbox or to a Public folder where it can be read by others.

Online Meeting Participant Sends the current workbook to one or more persons in a Microsoft NetMeeting conference.

Properties Displays information about the active workbook.

Exit Closes, or stops, the Microsoft Excel application.

Numbered File menu commands

Excel also lists as File menu commands the last four workbooks or workspaces you saved. You can open a listed workbook or workspace by choosing it from the File menu.

Edit Menu

Undo Reverses, or undoes, the last workbook change.

Repeat Duplicates the last workbook change.

Cut Moves the current workbook selection to the Clipboard.

Copy Moves a copy of the current workbook selection to the Clipboard.

Paste Moves the Clipboard contents to the active workbook.

Paste Special... Moves some portion of the Clipboard contents to the active workbook.

Paste As Hyperlink Moves the Clipboard contents to the active workbook and makes the newly pasted data a hyperlink.

Fill Displays the Fill submenu.

Down Copies contents of the selected column's top cell to the rest of the column.

Right Copies contents of the selected row's left cell to the rest of the row.

continues

Edit Menu *(continued)*

	Up	Copies contents of the selected column's bottom cell to the rest of the column.
	Left	Copies contents of the selected row's right cells to the rest of the row.
	Across Worksheets...	Copies contents of the selected group's first worksheet range to the rest of the group's worksheets.
	Series...	Describes a pattern of values or labels that Excel should use to fill the selected range.
	Justify	Arranges the active cell's text label so that it fits the selected range.
Clear	Displays the Clear submenu.	
	All	Erases contents, formats, and notes of selected cells.
	Formats	Erases formatting—numeric, alignment, fonts, and so on—of selected cells.
	Contents Del	Erases contents—labels, values, or formulas—of selected cells.
	Comments	Erases comments attached to selected cells.
Delete...	Removes the selected cell, column, or row from a worksheet.	
Delete Sheet	Removes the selected worksheet from a workbook.	
Move Or Copy Sheet...	Changes the current worksheet's position in a workbook or duplicates the current worksheet.	
Find...	Looks for cells matching a specified description.	
Replace...	Looks for cells matching a specified description and, optionally, replaces the contents.	
Go To...	Moves the cell selector to a specified location.	
Links...	Describes, updates, and changes a selected object's link.	
Object	Changes a selected object's border, background pattern, and protection.	

View Menu

Normal	Turns off Page Break Preview.
Page Break Preview	Displays a window showing where page breaks will fall in the printed worksheet, and allows you to adjust them.
Toolbars...	Adds, removes, and customizes toolbars.
Formula Bar	Turns off and on the display of the formula bar. (Command check box is selected if the formula bar is displayed.)
Status Bar	Turns off and on the display of the status bar. (Command check box is selected if the formula bar is displayed.)
Header And Footer...	Lets you add a custom header and footer to your workbooks.
Comments	Lets you add comments to selected cells.
Custom **V**iews...	Displays the Custom Views dialog box, allowing you to create and save custom views of the active worksheet.
F**u**ll Screen	Maximizes and restores the application and workbook windows. (Command check box is selected if the windows are maximized.)
Zoom...	Magnifies the workbook window by some specified percentage.

Insert Menu

Cells...	Adds cells to a row or to a column, or adds an entire row or column.
Rows	Adds a row to the active worksheet.
Columns	Adds a column to the active worksheet.
Worksheet	Adds a worksheet to the workbook.
C**h**art...	Starts the Chart Wizard.
Page **B**reak	Adds a page break to the left of the selected column or above the selected row.
Function...	Displays the Paste Function dialog box.
Name	Displays the Name submenu.
	Define... Lets you add and delete cell and range names.

continues

Insert Menu *(continued)*

Paste...	Lists cell and range names so that you can use one in a formula.
Create...	Creates cell names using labels stored in adjacent cells.
Apply...	Tells Excel to replace formula cell addresses with cell names.
Label...	Lets you add and delete label ranges.
Comment	Lets you attach a comment to the active cell.
Picture	Displays the Picture submenu.
Clip Art...	Displays the Insert ClipArt dialog box so that you can add clip art images to the worksheet.
From File...	Displays the Insert Picture dialog box so that you can insert a picture from a file on a disk.
AutoShapes	Displays the AutoShapes toolbar so that you can easily add interesting shapes and symbols to your workbook.
Organization Chart	Opens the Microsoft Organization Chart application so that you can add an organization chart to your worksheet.
WordArt...	Displays the WordArt Gallery dialog box so that you can add WordArt to your worksheet.
From Scanner Or Camera...	Opens the Microsoft Photo Editor application so that you can add scanned or digital photo images to your worksheets.
Map...	Activates the Data Map add-in so that you can chart geographical information.
Object...	Adds an embedded or a linked object to the active sheet.
Hyperlink...	Inserts a hyperlink to a World Wide Web site or to another file.

Format Menu

Cells...	Displays the Format Cells dialog box, letting you change a selected cell's/object's formatting, including alignment, font, border, pattern, and protection.

Row	Displays the Row submenu.
Height...	Changes a selected row's height.
AutoFit	Changes height of a selected row so that cell contents are fully visible.
Hide	Hides a selected row by making its height 0 points.
Unhide	Unhides hidden rows in a selection by restoring normal row height.
Column	Displays the Column submenu.
Width...	Changes width of a selected column.
AutoFit Selection	Changes width of a selected column so that all column entries are fully visible.
Hide	Hides the selected column by making its width 0.
Unhide	Unhides hidden columns in a selection by restoring the column's normal width.
Standard Width...	Changes width of all columns in the worksheet whose width has not been previously adjusted.
Sheet	Displays the Sheet submenu.
Rename	Changes the name of the active sheet.
Hide	Hides the active sheet.
Unhide...	Unhides hidden sheets in the selected group.
Background...	Adds a background pattern to the active worksheet.
AutoFormat...	Formats selected worksheet range by adding formatting for numbers, alignment, fonts, patterns, and borders.
Conditional Formatting...	Adds and deletes special formatting that applies only when cell contents meet certain conditions.
Style...	Adds, changes, and deletes formatting combinations called styles.

Tools Menu

Spelling...	Checks the spelling of words in the cell labels of the active worksheet.
AutoCorrect...	Adds AutoCorrection entries and specifies how AutoCorrect works.
Share Workbook...	Lists users working with a workbook, and describes what they can and can't do.
Track Changes	Displays the Track Changes submenu.

> **Highlight Changes...** Lets you set options to track revisions made to a workbook.

> **Accept Or Reject Changes...** Lets you review changes made to a workbook and decide which ones to accept or reject.

Merge Workbooks...	Lets you consolidate changes made to a workbook and decide which ones to accept or reject.
Protection	Displays the Protection submenu.

> **Protect Sheet.../Unprotect Sheet...** Prevents/allows changes to the active sheet and its contents.

> **Protect Workbook.../Unprotect Workbook...** Prevents/allows changes to workbook structure and workbook window.

> **Protect And Share Workbook...** Prevents/allows changes to shared workbook.

Online Collaboration	Displays the Online Collaboration submenu.

> **Meet Now** Launches Microsoft NetMeeting.

> **Schedule Meeting...** Opens an online meeting invitation in Microsoft Outlook.

> **Web Discussions** Displays the Web Discussion toolbar and connects with your discussion server.

Goal Seek...	Calculates input cell value required for formula to return target output value.
Scenarios...	Adds and uses what-if scenarios.
Auditing	Displays the Auditing submenu.

> **Trace Precedents** Draws a blue arrow to show the cells that supply input to the active cell's formula.

Trace Dependents Draws a blue arrow to show the cells with formulas that reference the active cell.

Trace Error Draws a thick red arrow from cells addressed by the selected cell formula returning an error, and a thin red arrow to cells with erroneous formulas that address the selected cell.

Remove All Arrows Erases the blue and red arrows drawn by the Auditing commands.

Show Auditing Toolbar Displays a toolbar of auditing tools.

Macro Displays the Macro submenu.

Macros Runs a macro.

Record New Macro Adds a macro sheet so that you can record a macro.

Security Controls the screening of macros for viruses.

Visual Basic Editor Opens a new project in Excel Visual Basic.

Microsoft Script Editor Writes or edits VBScript or JavaScript.

Add-Ins... Installs or uninstalls Excel add-ins.

Customize... Lets you control the availability and descriptions of toolbar buttons and menu commands.

Options Changes Excel's operation and appearance.

Data Menu

Sort... Sorts rows in a worksheet based on labels or values from one or more columns.

Filter Displays the Filter submenu.

AutoFilter Turns a list's headers into drop-down list boxes that you can use to selectively filter.

Show All Returns a filtered list to its previous, unfiltered condition.

Advanced Filter... Displays a dialog box you can use to specify filter criteria.

Form... Creates a form you can use to enter, edit, and delete rows of data in the worksheet.

continues

173

Data Menu *(continued)*

Sub̲totals...	Summarizes entries in the selected list.
Val̲idation...	Displays a dialog box allowing you to validate data entries in selected cells.
Ta̲ble...	Creates a what-if table.
Te̲xt To Columns...	Starts the Text Wizard, which you use to separate text into columns.
Co̲nsolidate...	Summarizes ranges of values in different worksheets.
G̲roup And Outline	Displays the Group And Outline submenu.

H̲ide Detail	Hides detail rows of the selected worksheet range.
S̲how Detail	Unhides previously hidden detail rows of the selected worksheet range.
G̲roup...	Groups selected cells in outline.
U̲ngroup...	Ungroups selected cells in outline.
A̲uto Outline	Creates an outline.
C̲lear Outline	Removes an outline.
Se̲ttings...	Creates or updates outline settings.

PivotTable and PivotChart Report...	Starts a wizard to help you create a PivotTable or PivotChart.
Get External D̲ata	Displays the Get External Data submenu.

Run Save̲d Query	Runs a previously created query.
New W̲eb Query	Creates a query to retrieve data from the World Wide Web and places the results in an Excel workbook.
N̲ew Database Query...	Creates a query to retrieve data from an external database query and places the results in an Excel workbook.
Import T̲ext File...	Retrieves data from an ASCII text file and places the results in an Excel workbook.
E̲dit Query...	Lets you edit an existing query.

Data Range Properties Lets you change how and when Excel refreshes data in an external database query.

Parameters... Lets you include Microsoft Access–type parameters in an external database query.

Refresh Data Updates a PivotTable's data with the most current worksheet data.

Window Menu

New Window Opens a new window for the active workbook.

Arrange... Rearranges the document windows into tiles or a cascading stack.

Hide Hides the active document window from view so that you can't see it.

Unhide... Displays a list of previously hidden windows so that you can unhide one.

Split/Remove Split Splits/unsplits the active document window.

Freeze/Unfreeze Panes If split, freezes or unfreezes the window panes above and to the left of the active cell.

Numbered Window menu commands

Excel also lists all the open document windows as numbered Window menu commands. You can open a listed window by choosing it from the Window menu.

Help Menu

Microsoft Excel Help Starts the Office Assistant.

Hide/Show The Office Assistant Hides the Office Assistant character or shows it, if hidden.

What's This? Displays helpful information about whatever you click next: a menu command, a toolbar button, or an element of the Excel application or document window.

Office On The Web If you have Internet access, connects you to a variety of Microsoft forums on the World Wide Web to get help with your questions.

continues

Help Menu *(continued)*

Lotus 1-2-3 Help...	Instructs how to accomplish a Lotus 1-2-3 task in Excel.
Detect And Repair...	Automatically finds and fixes problems with Excel.
About Microsoft Excel	Displays the copyright notice, the software version number, and your computer's available memory.

Toolbar Button Guide

Standard Toolbar

	Opens a new, blank workbook.
	Opens an existing workbook.
	Saves the active workbook on disk.
	E-mails the current workbook.
	Prints the active workbook on the default printer.
	Shows what the printed pages of a workbook will look like.
	Checks the spelling of words in the cell labels of the active workbook.
	Moves the current workbook selection to the Clipboard.
	Copies the current workbook selection to the Clipboard.
	Copies the Clipboard contents to the active workbook.
	Copies formatting of the active cell to other cells.
	Undoes the last workbook change.

Repeats the last workbook change.

Inserts a hyperlink to a World Wide Web site or to another file.

Sums worksheet selection, placing SUM functions in the selected cell.

Opens the Paste Function dialog box to apply one of Excel's built-in functions.

Uses the selected column to sort data in ascending value or A to Z alphabetic order.

Uses the selected column to sort data in descending value or Z to A reverse alphabetic order.

Starts the Chart Wizard.

Opens the add-in mapping application.

Displays the Drawing toolbar.

Magnifies or reduces workbook contents by the specified zoom percentage.

Displays and hides the Office Assistant.

Formatting Toolbar

Changes the font of the workbook selection.

Changes the character point size of the workbook selection.

Boldfaces characters in selected cells.

Italicizes characters in selected cells.

Underlines characters in selected cells.

continues

177

Formatting Toolbar *(continued)*

Left-aligns cell contents.

Centers cell contents.

Right-aligns cell contents.

Centers cell contents across selected columns.

Applies dollar sign, commas, and cents.

Converts decimal to percent, applies percent symbol.

Separates thousands with commas.

Adds one place to the right of the decimal point.

Removes one place from the right of the decimal point.

Decreases indent of the selection.

Increases indent of the selection.

Adds borders and lines.

Colors background and fills pattern of the selection.

Colors characters of the selection.

Chart Toolbar

Selects chart object to format.

Formats selected chart object.

Selects chart type to be plotted.

	Area chart
	3-D area chart
	3-D surface chart
	Bar chart
	3-D bar chart
	Radar chart
	Column chart
	3-D column chart
	Bubble chart
	Line chart
	3-D line, or ribbon, chart
	XY, or scatter, chart
	Pie chart
	3-D pie chart
	Doughnut chart
	3-D cylinder chart

continues

Chart Toolbar *(continued)*

	3-D cone chart
	3-D pyramid chart
	Adds and removes legends.
	Displays and hides table showing data the chart is based upon.
	Charts data by worksheet row.
	Charts data by worksheet column.
	Angles category axis text downward.
	Angles category axis text upward.

Chart Menu Guide

Chart Menu

Chart **T**ype...	Selects one of the 14 chart types.
Source Data...	Displays chart data range and series.
Chart **O**ptions...	Lets you add and edit chart titles, axes, gridlines, legend, labels, and table.
Location...	Lets you place a chart as a new sheet or as an object on an existing worksheet.
Add Data...	Lets you add data to a chart.
Add T**r**endline...	Lets you add a trendline to a chart.
3-D **V**iew...	Adjusts a 3-D chart's elevation, rotation, or height.

Chart menu commands

When a chart is active, Excel adds the Chart menu and its commands to the regular menu bar.

The manuscript for this book was prepared and submitted to Microsoft Press in electronic form. Text files were prepared using Microsoft Word 97. Pages were composed by Stephen L. Nelson, Inc., using PageMaker 6.5 for Windows, with text in Minion and display type in Univers. Composed pages were delivered to the printer as electronic prepress files.

Cover Designer
Tim Girvin Design, Inc.

Layout
Stefan Knorr

Project Editor
Paula Thurman

Writer
Steve Nelson

Technical Editor
Brian Milbrath

Indexer
Julie Kawabata

Printed on recycled paper stock.

Stay in the *running* for maximum productivity.

These are *the* answer books for business users of Microsoft Office 2000. They are packed with everything from quick, clear instructions for new users to comprehensive answers for power users—the authoritative reference to keep by your computer and use every day. THE RUNNING SERIES—learning solutions made by Microsoft.

- RUNNING MICROSOFT® EXCEL 2000
- RUNNING MICROSOFT OFFICE 2000 PREMIUM
- RUNNING MICROSOFT OFFICE 2000 PROFESSIONAL
- RUNNING MICROSOFT OFFICE 2000 SMALL BUSINESS EDITION
- RUNNING MICROSOFT WORD 2000
- RUNNING MICROSOFT POWERPOINT® 2000
- RUNNING MICROSOFT ACCESS 2000
- RUNNING MICROSOFT INTERNET EXPLORER 5.0
- RUNNING MICROSOFT FRONTPAGE®
- RUNNING MICROSOFT OUTLOOK® 2000

Microsoft®

mspress.microsoft.com

See clearly—
now!

Here's the remarkable, *visual* way to quickly find answers about the powerfully integrated features of the Microsoft® Office 2000 applications. Microsoft Press AT A GLANCE books let you focus on particular tasks and show you, with clear, numbered steps, the easiest way to get them done right now. Put Office 2000 to work today, with AT A GLANCE learning solutions, made by Microsoft.

- MICROSOFT OFFICE 2000 PROFESSIONAL AT A GLANCE
- MICROSOFT WORD 2000 AT A GLANCE
- MICROSOFT EXCEL 2000 AT A GLANCE
- MICROSOFT POWERPOINT® 2000 AT A GLANCE
- MICROSOFT ACCESS 2000 AT A GLANCE
- MICROSOFT FRONTPAGE® 2000 AT A GLANCE
- MICROSOFT PUBLISHER 2000 AT A GLANCE
- MICROSOFT OFFICE 2000 SMALL BUSINESS AT A GLANCE
- MICROSOFT PHOTODRAW® 2000 AT A GLANCE
- MICROSOFT INTERNET EXPLORER 5 AT A GLANCE
- MICROSOFT OUTLOOK® 2000 AT A GLANCE

Microsoft®

mspress.microsoft.com